THE LIBRARY
OF
THE UNIVERSITY
OF CALIFORNIA
LOS ANGELES

ISBN: 9781290441162

Published by:
HardPress Publishing
8345 NW 66TH ST #2561
MIAMI FL 33166-2626

Email: info@hardpress.net
Web: http://www.hardpress.net

The Intruder

THE BLIND
THE SEVEN PRINCESSES
THE DEATH OF TINTAGILES

BY
MAURICE MAETERLINCK

Translated by
RICHARD HOVEY

NEW YORK
DODD, MEAD AND COMPANY
1914

COPYRIGHT, 1894, 1896, BY
STONE AND KIMBALL

Contents

	PAGE
THE INTRUDER	9
THE BLIND	57
THE SEVEN PRINCESSES	117
THE DEATH OF TINTAGILES	167

Persons.

The Grandfather. (*He is blind.*)
The Father.
The Uncle.
The Three Daughters.
The Sister of Charity.
The Maid-servant.

The scene in modern times.

The Intruder

To Edmond Picard

The Intruder.

[A gloomy room in an old château. A door on the right, a door on the left, and a small secret door in one corner. At the back, stained-glass windows, in which green is the dominant color, and a glass door opening upon a terrace. A big Dutch clock in a corner. A lighted lamp.]

THE THREE DAUGHTERS.

Come here, grandfather. Sit under the lamp.

THE GRANDFATHER.

It seems to me it is not very light here.

THE FATHER.

Shall we go out on the terrace, or shall we stay in the room?

THE UNCLE.

Would n't it be better to stay here? It has rained all the week, and the nights are damp and cold.

THE ELDEST DAUGHTER.

The stars are out, though.

THE UNCLE.

Oh, the stars — that makes no difference.

THE GRANDFATHER.

We had better stay here. You don't know what may happen.

THE FATHER.

We need have no more anxiety. She is out of danger. . . .

THE GRANDFATHER.

I believe she is not doing well.

THE FATHER.

Why do you say that?

THE GRANDFATHER.

I have heard her voice.

THE FATHER.

But since the doctors assure us that we may be easy. . . .

THE UNCLE.

You know quite well your father-in-law likes to alarm us needlessly.

THE GRANDFATHER.

I do not see things as you do.

THE UNCLE.

Then you should trust to us, who do see. She was looking very well this afternoon. She is sleeping quietly now; and we are not going needlessly to poison the first pleasant evening fortune gives us. . . . It seems to me we have a right to rest, and even to laugh a little, without being afraid, this evening.

THE FATHER.

That is true ; this is the first time I have felt at home, as if I were in my own household, since this terrible child-birth.

THE UNCLE.

Once sickness enters a house, it is as if there were a stranger in the family.

THE FATHER.

And then, you see, too, outside the family, you can count on no one.

THE UNCLE.

You are quite right.

THE GRANDFATHER.

Why could n't I see my poor daughter to-day?

THE UNCLE.

You know very well that the doctor forbade it

THE GRANDFATHER.

I do not know what to think.

THE UNCLE.

It is useless to alarm yourself.

THE GRANDFATHER.

[*Pointing to the door on the left.*] She cannot hear us?

THE FATHER.

We will not speak loudly enough; besides, the door is very thick, and then the Sister of Charity is with her, and will warn us if we are making too much noise.

THE GRANDFATHER.

[*Pointing to the door on the right.*] He cannot hear us?

THE FATHER.

No, no.

THE GRANDFATHER.

He sleeps?

THE FATHER.

I suppose so.

THE GRANDFATHER.

We ought to go and see.

The Intruder.

THE UNCLE.

He would give me more anxiety than your wife, this little fellow. It is several weeks since he was born, and he has hardly moved; he has not uttered a single cry yet; you would say he was a wax baby.

THE GRANDFATHER.

I believe he will be deaf, and perhaps dumb. . . . That is what comes of marrying cousins. . . . [*Reproachful silence.*

THE FATHER.

I am almost angry with him for the suffering he has caused his mother.

THE UNCLE.

You must be reasonable; it is not the poor little fellow's fault. — He is all alone in that room?

THE FATHER.

Yes; the doctor no longer allows him to remain in his mother's room.

THE UNCLE.

But the nurse is with him?

THE FATHER.

No; she has gone to rest a moment; she has well earned it these last few days. — Ursula, just run and see if he is asleep.

THE ELDEST DAUGHTER.

Yes, father.

[The three sisters get up, and go into the room on the right, hand in hand.]

THE FATHER.

At what time is our sister coming?

THE UNCLE.

About nine o'clock, I believe.

THE FATHER.

It is after nine. I would have liked her to come this evening; my wife was quite bent on seeing her.

THE UNCLE.

She is sure to come. Is it the first time she has ever come here?

THE FATHER.

She has never entered the house.

THE UNCLE.

It is very difficult for her to leave her convent.

THE FATHER.

She will be alone?

THE UNCLE.

I think one of the nuns will accompany her. They cannot go out alone.

THE FATHER.
She is the Superior, though.

THE UNCLE.
The rule is the same for all.

THE GRANDFATHER.
You are no longer anxious?

THE UNCLE.
Why should we be anxious? There is no need to keep returning to that? There is nothing more to fear.

THE GRANDFATHER.
Your sister is older than you?

THE UNCLE.
She is the eldest of us all.

THE GRANDFATHER.
I do not know what ails me; I feel uneasy. I wish your sister were here.

THE UNCLE.
She will come; she promised to.

THE GRANDFATHER.
I wish this evening were over!
[The Three Daughters come in again.]

THE FATHER.

He sleeps?

THE ELDEST DAUGHTER.

Yes, father; very soundly.

THE UNCLE.

What shall we do while we are waiting?

THE GRANDFATHER.

Waiting for what?

THE UNCLE.

Waiting for our sister.

THE FATHER.

You see nothing coming, Ursula?

THE ELDEST DAUGHTER.

[*At the window.*]   No, father.

THE FATHER.

And in the avenue? — You see the avenue?

THE DAUGHTER.

Yes, father; it is moonlight, and I see the avenue as far as the cypress wood.

THE GRANDFATHER.

And you see no one, Ursula?

THE DAUGHTER.

No one, grandfather.

The Intruder.

THE UNCLE.

How is the weather?

THE DAUGHTER.

Very fine. Do you hear the nightingales?

THE UNCLE.

Yes, yes!

THE DAUGHTER.

A little wind is rising in the avenue.

THE GRANDFATHER.

A little wind in the avenue, Ursula?

THE DAUGHTER.

Yes; the trees are stirring a little.

THE UNCLE.

It is surprising that my sister should not be here yet.

THE GRANDFATHER.

I do not hear the nightingales any longer, Ursula.

THE DAUGHTER.

I believe some one has come into the garden, grandfather.

THE GRANDFATHER.

Who is it?

THE DAUGHTER.

I do not know; I see no one.

THE UNCLE.

Because there is no one there.

THE DAUGHTER.

There must be some one in the garden; the nightingales are silent all at once.

THE GRANDFATHER.

I hear no footsteps, though.

THE DAUGHTER.

It must be that some one is passing near the pond, for the swans are frightened.

ANOTHER DAUGHTER.

All the fish of the pond are rising suddenly.

THE FATHER.

You see no one?

THE DAUGHTER.

No one, father.

THE FATHER.

But yet the pond is in the moonlight. . . .

THE DAUGHTER.

Yes; I can see that the swans are frightened.

THE UNCLE.

I am sure it is my sister that frightens them. She must have come in by the little gate.

THE FATHER.

I cannot understand why the dogs do not bark.

THE DAUGHTER.

I see the watch-dog in the back of his kennel. — The swans are crossing to the other bank! . . .

THE UNCLE.

They are afraid of my sister. I will go and see. [*He calls.*] Sister! sister! Is it you? — There is no one there.

THE DAUGHTER.

I am sure that some one has come into the garden. You will see.

THE UNCLE.

But she would answer me.

THE GRANDFATHER.

Are not the nightingales beginning to sing again, Ursula?

THE DAUGHTER.

I no longer hear a single one in all the fields.

THE GRANDFATHER.
And yet there is no noise.

THE FATHER.
There is a stillness of death.

THE GRANDFATHER.
It must be some stranger that frightens them, for if it were one of the household, they would not be silent.

THE DAUGHTER.
There is one on the big weeping willow. — It has flown away! . . .

THE UNCLE.
Are you going to talk about nightingales all night?

THE GRANDFATHER.
Are all the windows open, Ursula?

THE DAUGHTER.
The glass door is open, grandfather.

THE GRANDFATHER.
It seems to me that the cold comes into the room.

THE DAUGHTER.
There is a little wind in the garden, grandfather, and the rose leaves are falling.

The Intruder.

THE FATHER.

Well, shut the door, Ursula. It is late.

THE DAUGHTER.

Yes, father. — I cannot shut the door, father.

THE TWO OTHER DAUGHTERS.

We cannot shut the door.

THE GRANDFATHER.

Why, children, what is the matter with the door?

THE UNCLE.

You need not say that in such an extraordinary voice. I will go and help them.

THE ELDEST DAUGHTER.

We do not quite succeed in closing it.

THE UNCLE.

It is because of the damp. Let us all push together. . . . There must be something between the doors.

THE FATHER.

The carpenter will set it right to-morrow.

THE GRANDFATHER.

Is the carpenter coming to-morrow?

THE DAUGHTER.

Yes, grandfather; he is coming to work in the cellar.

THE GRANDFATHER.

He will make a noise in the house! . . .

THE DAUGHTER.

I will tell him to work quietly.

> [All at once the sound of the sharpening of a scythe is heard outside.]

THE GRANDFATHER.

[*Startled.*] Oh!

THE UNCLE.

Ursula, what is that?

THE DAUGHTER.

I don't quite know; I think it is the gardener. I cannot see very well; he is in the shadow of the house.

THE FATHER.

It is the gardener going to mow.

THE UNCLE.

He mows by night?

THE FATHER.

Is not to-morrow Sunday? — Yes. — I noticed that the grass was very high about the house.

THE GRANDFATHER.

It seems to me his scythe makes as much noise —

THE DAUGHTER.

He is mowing near the house.

THE GRANDFATHER.

Can you see him, Ursula?

THE DAUGHTER.

No, grandfather; he is in the dark.

THE GRANDFATHER.

It seems to me his scythe makes as much noise —

THE DAUGHTER.

That is because you have a very sensitive ear, grandfather.

THE GRANDFATHER.

I am afraid he will wake my daughter.

THE UNCLE.

We hardly hear him.

THE GRANDFATHER.

I hear him as if he were mowing in the house.

THE UNCLE.

She will not hear it; there is no danger.

THE FATHER.

It seems to me the lamp is not burning well this evening.

THE UNCLE.

It wants filling.

THE FATHER.

I saw it filled this morning. It has burnt badly ever since the window was shut.

THE UNCLE.

I think the chimney is dim.

THE FATHER.

It will burn better soon.

THE DAUGHTER.

Grandfather is asleep. He has not slept before for three nights.

THE FATHER.

He has been very worried.

THE UNCLE.

He always worries too much. There are times when he will not listen to reason.

THE FATHER.

It is quite excusable at his age.

THE UNCLE.

God knows what we shall be like at his age!

THE FATHER.
He is nearly eighty years old.

THE UNCLE.
Well, then, he has a right to be strange.

THE FATHER.
Perhaps we shall be stranger than he is.

THE UNCLE.
One does not know what may happen. He is odd sometimes.

THE FATHER.
He is like all the blind.

THE UNCLE.
They reflect too much.

THE FATHER.
They have too much time to spare.

THE UNCLE.
They have nothing else to do.

THE FATHER.
And, besides, they have no amusements.

THE UNCLE.
That must be terrible.

THE FATHER.

It seems they get used to it.

THE UNCLE.

I cannot imagine that.

THE FATHER.

They are certainly to be pitied.

THE UNCLE.

Not to know where one is, not to know whence one has come, not to know whither one is going, no longer to distinguish midday from midnight, nor summer from winter. . . . And always that darkness, that darkness! . . . I would rather not live. . . . Is it absolutely incurable?

THE FATHER.

It appears so.

THE UNCLE.

But he is not absolutely blind?

THE FATHER.

He can distinguish a strong light.

THE UNCLE.

Let us take care of our poor eyes.

THE FATHER.

He often has strange ideas.

THE UNCLE.

There are times when he is not amusing.

THE FATHER.

He says absolutely everything he thinks.

THE UNCLE.

But formerly he was not like this?

THE FATHER.

No; formerly he was as rational as we are; he never said anything extraordinary. It is true, Ursula encourages him a little too much; she answers all his questions —

THE UNCLE.

It would be better not to answer. It's a mistaken kindness to him. [*Ten o'clock strikes.*

THE GRANDFATHER.

[*Waking up.*] Am I facing the glass door?

THE DAUGHTER.

You have had a good sleep, grandfather?

THE GRANDFATHER.

Am I facing the glass door?

THE DAUGHTER.

Yes, grandfather.

THE GRANDFATHER.

There is no one at the glass door?

THE DAUGHTER.

No, grandfather; I see no one.

THE GRANDFATHER.

I thought some one was waiting. No one has come, Ursula?

THE DAUGHTER.

No one, grandfather.

THE GRANDFATHER.

[*To the* UNCLE *and* FATHER.] And your sister has not come?

THE UNCLE.

It is too late; she will not come now. It is not nice of her.

THE FATHER.

I begin to be anxious about her.
[A noise, as of some one coming into the house.]

THE UNCLE.

She is here! Did you hear?

THE FATHER.

Yes; some one has come in at the basement.

The Intruder.

THE UNCLE.

It must be our sister. I recognized her step.

THE GRANDFATHER.

I heard slow footsteps.

THE FATHER.

She came in very softly.

THE UNCLE.

She knows there is sickness. . . .

THE GRANDFATHER.

I hear nothing more now.

THE UNCLE.

She will come up immediately; they will tell her we are here.

THE FATHER.

I am glad she has come.

THE UNCLE.

I was sure she would come this evening.

THE GRANDFATHER.

She is a long time coming up.

THE UNCLE.

However, it must be she.

THE FATHER.

We are not expecting any one else.

THE GRANDFATHER.

I hear no noise in the basement.

THE FATHER.

I will call the maid. We must know what to expect. [*He pulls the bell-rope.*

THE GRANDFATHER.

I hear a noise on the stairs already.

THE FATHER.

It is the maid coming up.

THE GRANDFATHER.

It seems to me she is not alone.

THE FATHER.

It is because the maid makes so much noise. . . .

THE GRANDFATHER.

It seems to me she is not alone.

THE FATHER.

She is getting terribly stout; I believe she is dropsical.

THE UNCLE.

It is time you got rid of her; you will have her on your hands.

THE GRANDFATHER.

I hear your sister's step!

THE FATHER.

I hear no one but the maid.

THE GRANDFATHER.

It is your sister! It is your sister!
[*A knock at the secret door.*

THE UNCLE.

She is knocking at the door of the private stairway.

THE FATHER.

I will go open it myself, because that little door makes too much noise; it is only used when we want to come up without being seen. [*He partly opens the little door;* the MAID-SERVANT *remains outside in the opening.*] Where are you?

THE MAID-SERVANT.

Here, sir.

THE GRANDFATHER.

Your sister is at the door.

THE UNCLE.

I see no one but the maid.

THE FATHER.

There is no one there but the maid. [*To the* MAID-SERVANT.] Who was it who came into the house?

THE MAID-SERVANT.

Came into the house, sir?

THE FATHER.

Yes; some one came just now?

THE SERVANT.

No one came, sir.

THE GRANDFATHER.

Who is it sighs so?

THE UNCLE.

It is the maid; she is out of breath.

THE GRANDFATHER.

Is she crying?

THE UNCLE.

Why, no; why should she be crying?

THE FATHER.

[*To the* MAID-SERVANT.] No one came in just now?

THE MAID-SERVANT.

No, sir.

THE FATHER.

But we heard the door open!

THE MAID-SERVANT.

It was I shutting the door, sir.

THE FATHER.

It was open?

THE MAID-SERVANT.

Yes, sir.

THE FATHER.

Why was it open, at this hour?

THE MAID-SERVANT.

I do not know, sir. *I* had shut it.

THE FATHER.

But then who was it opened it?

THE MAID-SERVANT.

I do not know, sir. Some one must have gone out after me, sir.

THE FATHER.

You must be careful. — Don't push the door; you know what a noise it makes!

THE MAID-SERVANT.

But **I** am not touching the door, sir.

THE FATHER.

But you are. You push as if you were trying to get into the room.

THE MAID-SERVANT.

But I am three steps away from the door, sir.

THE FATHER.

Don't talk quite so loudly.

THE GRANDFATHER.

Are you putting out the light?

THE ELDEST DAUGHTER.

No, grandfather.

THE GRANDFATHER.

It seems to me it is dark all at once.

THE FATHER.

[*To the* MAID-SERVANT.] You may go down now; but do not make so much noise on the stairs.

THE MAID-SERVANT.

I did not make any noise on the stairs, sir.

THE FATHER.

I tell you, you made a noise. Go down softly; you will wake your mistress.

THE MAID-SERVANT.

It was not I who made a noise, sir.

THE FATHER.

And if any one comes now, say that we are not at home.

THE UNCLE.

Yes; say that we are not at home.

THE GRANDFATHER.

[*Shuddering.*]   You must not say that!

THE FATHER.

. . . Except to my sister and the doctor.

THE UNCLE.

When will the doctor come?

THE FATHER.

He will not be able to come before midnight.
   [He shuts the door. A clock is heard striking eleven.]

THE GRANDFATHER.

She has come in?

THE FATHER.

Who, pray?

THE GRANDFATHER.

The maid.

THE FATHER.

Why, no; she has gone downstairs.

THE GRANDFATHER.

I thought she was sitting at the table.

THE UNCLE.

The maid?

THE GRANDFATHER.

Yes.

THE UNCLE.

Well, that's all that was lacking

THE GRANDFATHER.

No one has come into the room?

THE FATHER.

Why no; no one has come in.

THE GRANDFATHER.

And your sister is not here?

THE UNCLE.

Our sister has not come. Where have your thoughts wandered?

THE GRANDFATHER.

You want to deceive me.

THE UNCLE.

Deceive you?

THE GRANDFATHER.

Ursula, tell me the truth, for the love of God!

THE ELDEST DAUGHTER.

Grandfather! Grandfather! what is the matter with you?

THE GRANDFATHER.

Something has happened! . . . I am sure my daughter is worse! . . .

THE UNCLE.

Are you dreaming?

THE GRANDFATHER.

You do not want to tell me! . . . I see plainly there is something! . . .

THE UNCLE.

In that case you see better than we.

THE GRANDFATHER.

Ursula, tell me the truth.

THE DAUGHTER.

But we are telling you the truth, grandfather!

THE GRANDFATHER.

You are not speaking in your natural voice.

THE FATHER.

That is because you frighten her.

THE GRANDFATHER.

Your voice is changed, — yours, too!

THE FATHER.

But you are going mad!

[He and the Uncle make signs to each other that the Grandfather has lost his reason.]

THE GRANDFATHER.

I hear plainly that you are afraid.

THE FATHER.

But what should we be afraid of?

THE GRANDFATHER.

Why do you want to deceive me?

THE UNCLE.

Who thinks of deceiving you?

THE GRANDFATHER.

Why have you put out the light?

THE UNCLE.

But the light has not been put out; it is as light as before.

THE DAUGHTER.

It seems to me the lamp has gone down.

THE FATHER.

I see as well as usual.

THE GRANDFATHER.

I have millstones on my eyes! Children, tell me what is happening here! Tell me, for the love of God, you who can see! I am here, all alone, in darkness without end! I do not know who seats himself beside me! I do not know what is happening two steps from me! . . . Why were you speaking in a low voice just now?

THE FATHER.

No one spoke in a low voice.

THE GRANDFATHER.

You spoke in a low voice at the door.

THE FATHER.

You heard all I said.

THE GRANDFATHER.

You brought some one into the room.

THE FATHER.

But I tell you no one has come in!

THE GRANDFATHER.

Is it your sister or a priest? — You must not try to deceive me. — Ursula, who was it that came in?

THE DAUGHTER.

No one, grandfather.

THE GRANDFATHER.

You must not try to deceive me; I know what I know! — How many are we here?

THE DAUGHTER.

There are six of us about the table, grandfather.

THE GRANDFATHER.

You are all about the table?

THE DAUGHTER.

Yes, grandfather.

THE GRANDFATHER.

You are there, Paul?

THE FATHER.

Yes.

THE GRANDFATHER.

You are there, Oliver?

THE UNCLE.

Why, yes; why, yes; I am here, in my usual place. This is not serious, is it?

THE GRANDFATHER.

You are there, Geneviève?

ONE OF THE DAUGHTERS.

Yes, grandfather.

THE GRANDFATHER.

You are there, Gertrude?

ANOTHER DAUGHTER.

Yes, grandfather.

THE GRANDFATHER.

You are here, Ursula?

THE ELDEST DAUGHTER.

Yes, grandfather, by your side.

THE GRANDFATHER.

And who is that sitting there?

THE DAUGHTER.

Where do you mean, grandfather? — There is no one.

THE GRANDFATHER.

There, there — in the midst of us!

THE DAUGHTER.

But there is no one, grandfather.

THE FATHER.

We tell you there is no one!

THE GRANDFATHER.

But you do not see, any of you!

THE UNCLE.

Oh, come now; you are joking.

THE GRANDFATHER.

I have no wish to joke, I can assure you.

THE UNCLE.

Well, then, believe those that see.

THE GRANDFATHER.

[*Undecidedly.*] I thought there was some one. . . . I believe I shall not live much longer. . . .

THE UNCLE.

Why should we go to work to deceive you? What good would that do?

THE FATHER.

We ought clearly to tell you the truth.

THE UNCLE.

What good would it do to deceive each other?

THE FATHER.

You could not live long without finding it out.

THE GRANDFATHER.

I wish I were at home!

THE FATHER.

But you are at home here!

The Intruder.

THE UNCLE.

Are we not at home?

THE FATHER.

Are you among strangers?

THE UNCLE.

You are strange this evening.

THE GRANDFATHER.

It is you who seem strange to me!

THE FATHER.

Do you want anything?

THE GRANDFATHER.

I do not know what ails me.

THE UNCLE.

Will you take anything?

THE ELDEST DAUGHTER.

Grandfather! grandfather! What do you want, grandfather?

THE GRANDFATHER.

Give me your little hands, my children.

THE THREE DAUGHTERS.

Yes, grandfather.

THE GRANDFATHER.
Why are you all three trembling, my children?

THE ELDEST DAUGHTER.
We are hardly trembling at all, grandfather.

THE GRANDFATHER.
I believe you are all three pale.

THE ELDEST DAUGHTER.
It is late, grandfather, and we are tired.

THE FATHER.
You must go to bed, and grandfather too would do better to take a little rest.

THE GRANDFATHER.
I could not sleep to-night!

THE UNCLE.
We will wait for the doctor.

THE GRANDFATHER.
Prepare me for the truth!

THE UNCLE.
But there is no truth!

THE GRANDFATHER.
Then I do not know what there is!

THE UNCLE.

I tell you there is nothing at all!

THE GRANDFATHER.

I would like to see my poor daughter!

THE FATHER.

But you know very well that is impossible; she must not be wakened needlessly.

THE UNCLE.

You will see her to-morrow.

THE GRANDFATHER.

We hear no sound in her room.

THE UNCLE.

I should be uneasy if I heard any sound.

THE GRANDFATHER.

It is very long since I saw my daughter. . . . I took her hands yesterday evening, but I could not see her! . . . I no longer know what she is becoming. . . . I no longer know how she is. . . . I am no longer familiar with her face. . . . She must have changed in these weeks! . . . I felt the little bones of her cheeks under my hands. . . . There is nothing but the darkness between her and me, and all of you! . . . This is not life — this is not living! . . . You sit there, all of you, with open eyes that look at my dead eyes, and not one of you has pity ! . . . I do not know what ails me. . . . No one tells what ought to be told me. . . . And everything is terrifying when you dream of it ! . . . But why do you not speak?

THE UNCLE.

What would you have us say, since you will not believe us?

THE GRANDFATHER.

You are afraid of betraying yourselves !

THE FATHER.

Do be reasonable now.

THE GRANDFATHER.

For a long time something has been hidden from me here ! . . . Something has happened in the house. . . . But I begin to understand now. . . . I have been deceived too long ! — You think, then, that I shall never find out anything? — There are moments when I am less blind than you, you know ! . . . Have I not heard you whispering, for days and days, as if you were in the house of some one who had hanged himself? — I dare not say what I know this evening. . . . But I will know the truth ! I shall wait for you to tell me the truth ; but I have known it for a long time, in spite of you ! — And now, I feel that you are all as pale as the dead !

THE THREE DAUGHTERS.

Grandfather! grandfather! What is the matter, grandfather?

THE GRANDFATHER.

It is not of you that I speak, my children; no, it is not of you that I speak. . . . I know quite well you would tell me the truth, if they were not by! . . . And besides, I am sure they are deceiving you also. . . . You will see, children, you will see! . . . Do I not hear all three of you sobbing?

THE UNCLE.

For my part, I will not stay here.

THE FATHER.

Can my wife really be so ill?

THE GRANDFATHER.

You need not try to deceive me any longer; it is too late now, and I know the truth better than you! . . .

THE UNCLE.

But after all we are not blind, are we?

THE FATHER.

Would you like to go into your daughter's room? There is a mistake here and a misunderstanding that should end. — Would you? . . .

THE GRANDFATHER.

No, no; not now . . . not yet. . . .

THE UNCLE.

You see plainly, you are not reasonable.

THE GRANDFATHER.

One never knows all that a man has been unable to say in his life! . . . Who was it made that noise?

THE ELDEST DAUGHTER.

It is the flickering of the lamp, grandfather.

THE GRANDFATHER.

It seems to me it is very unsteady — very unsteady.

THE DAUGHTER.

It is the cold wind that vexes it . . . it is the cold wind that vexes it. ... .

THE UNCLE.

There is no cold wind, the windows are shut.

THE DAUGHTER.

I think it is going out.

THE FATHER.

The oil must be out.

THE DAUGHTER.

It has gone entirely out.

THE FATHER.

We cannot stay like this in the dark.

THE UNCLE.

Why not? I am already accustomed to it.

THE FATHER.

There is a light in my wife's room.

THE UNCLE.

We will take it by and by, when the doctor has come.

THE FATHER.

It is true, we see well enough; there is light from outside.

THE GRANDFATHER.

Is it light outside?

THE FATHER.

Lighter than here.

THE UNCLE.

For my part, I would as soon talk in the dark.

THE FATHER.

So would I. [*Silence.*

THE GRANDFATHER.

It seems to me the clock makes such a noise ! . . .

THE ELDEST DAUGHTER.

That is because we are not speaking now, grandfather.

THE GRANDFATHER.

But why are you all silent?

THE UNCLE.

Of what would you have us speak? — You are not in earnest to-night.

THE GRANDFATHER.

Is it very dark in the room?

THE UNCLE.

It is not very light. [*Silence.*

THE GRANDFATHER.

I do not feel well, Ursula; open the window a little.

THE FATHER.

Yes, daughter; open the window a little; I begin to feel the want of air myself.

[The girl opens the window.

THE UNCLE.

I positively believe we have stayed shut up too long.

The Intruder.

THE GRANDFATHER.

Is the window open, Ursula?

THE DAUGHTER.

Yes, grandfather; it is wide open.

THE GRANDFATHER.

One would not have said it was open; there is not a sound outside.

THE DAUGHTER.

No, grandfather; there is not the least sound.

THE FATHER.

The silence is extraordinary!

THE DAUGHTER.

One could hear an angel's step.

THE UNCLE.

That is the reason I do not like the country.

THE GRANDFATHER.

I wish I could hear some sound. What time is it, Ursula?

THE DAUGHTER.

Almost midnight, grandfather.

    [Here the Uncle begins to walk up and down the room.]

THE GRANDFATHER.

Who is it walking around like that?

THE UNCLE.

It is I! it is I! Do not be frightened! I feel the need of walking a little. [*Silence.*] — But I am going to sit down again, — I do not see where I am going. [*Silence.*

THE GRANDFATHER.

I wish I were somewhere else!

THE DAUGHTER.

Where would you like to go, grandfather?

THE GRANDFATHER.

I do not know where, — into another room — no matter where! no matter where! . . .

THE FATHER.

Where should we go?

THE UNCLE.

It is too late to go anywhere else.

[Silence. They are sitting motionless, round the table.]

THE GRANDFATHER.

What is that I hear, Ursula?

THE DAUGHTER.

Nothing, grandfather; it is the leaves falling. Yes, it is the leaves falling on the terrace.

THE GRANDFATHER.

Go shut the window, Ursula.

THE DAUGHTER.

Yes, grandfather.

[She shuts the window, comes back, and sits down.]

THE GRANDFATHER.

I am cold. [*Silence. The three sisters kiss each other.*] What is it I hear now?

THE FATHER.

It is the three sisters kissing each other.

THE UNCLE.

It seems to me they are very pale this evening. [*Silence.*

THE GRANDFATHER.

What is it I hear now, Ursula?

THE DAUGHTER.

Nothing, grandfather; it is the clasping of my hands. [*Silence.*

THE GRANDFATHER.

What is it I hear? what is it I hear, Ursula?

THE DAUGHTER.

I do not know, grandfather; perhaps my sisters — they are trembling a little.

THE GRANDFATHER.

I am afraid, too, my children.

> [Here a ray of moonlight penetrates through a corner of the stained glass, and spreads strange gleams here and there in the room. Midnight strikes, and at the last stroke it seems to some that a sound is heard, very vaguely, as of some one rising in all haste.]

THE GRANDFATHER.

[*Shuddering with peculiar horror.*]   Who is it that rose?

THE UNCLE.

No one rose!

THE FATHER.

I did not rise!

THE THREE DAUGHTERS.

Nor I! . . . Nor I! . . . Nor I!

THE GRANDFATHER.

Some one rose from the table!

THE UNCLE.

Light the lamp!

> [Here suddenly a wail of fright is heard in the child's room, on the right; and this wail continues, with gradations of terror until the end of the scene.]

THE FATHER.

Listen! the child!

THE UNCLE.

He has never cried before!

THE FATHER.

Let us go and look!

THE UNCLE.

The light! The light!

[At this moment a hurrying of headlong heavy steps is heard in the room on the left. — Then a deathly stillness. — They listen in a dumb terror, until the door opens slowly, and the light from the next room falls into that in which they are waiting. The Sister of Charity appears on the threshold, in the black garments of her order, and bows as she makes the sign of the cross, to announce the death of the wife. They understand, and, after a moment of hesitation and fright, silently enter the chamber of death, while the Uncle politely effaces himself at the doorstep, to let the three young girls pass. The blind man, left alone, rises and gropes excitedly about the table in the darkness.

THE GRANDFATHER.

Where are you going? — Where are you going? — My children! — They have left me all alone!

[CURTAIN.]

The Blind.

To Charles Van Lerberghe.

Persons.

THE PRIEST.
THREE MEN WHO WERE BORN BLIND.
A VERY OLD BLIND MAN.
FIFTH BLIND MAN (*who is also deaf*).
SIXTH BLIND MAN (*who can distinguish light and darkness*).
THREE OLD BLIND WOMEN IN PRAYER.
A VERY OLD BLIND WOMAN.
A YOUNG BLIND GIRL.
A BLIND MADWOMAN.
AN INFANT, *child of the* MADWOMAN.
A DOG.

The Blind.

—◆—

[An ancient Norland forest, with an eternal look, under a sky of deep stars.

In the centre, and in the deep of the night, a very old priest is sitting, wrapped in a great black cloak. The chest and the head, gently upturned and deathly motionless, rest against the trunk of a giant hollow oak. The face is fearsome pale and of an immovable waxen lividness, in which the purple lips fall slightly apart. The dumb, fixed eyes no longer look out from the visible side of Eternity and seem to bleed with immemorial sorrows and with tears. The hair, of a solemn whiteness, falls in stringy locks, stiff and few, over a face more illuminated and more weary than all that surrounds it in the watchful stillness of that melancholy wood. The hands, pitifully thin, are clasped rigidly over the thighs.

On the right, six old men, all blind, are sitting on stones, stumps and dead leaves.

On the left, separated from them by an uprooted tree and fragments of rock, six women, also blind, are sitting opposite the old men. Three among them pray and mourn without ceasing, in a muffled voice. Another is old in the extreme. The fifth, in an attitude of mute insanity, holds on her knees a little sleeping child. The sixth is strangely young, and her whole body is drenched with her beautiful hair. They, as well as the old men, are all clad in the same ample and sombre garments. Most of them are waiting, with their elbows on their knees and their faces in their hands; and all seem to have lost the habit of ineffectual gesture and no longer turn their heads at the stifled and uneasy noises of the Island. Tall funereal trees, — yews, weeping-willows, cypresses, — cover them with their faithful shadows. A cluster of long, sickly asphodels is in bloom, not far from the priest, in the night. It is unusually oppressive, despite the moonlight that here and there struggles to pierce for an instant the glooms of the foliage.]

FIRST BLIND MAN (*who was born blind*).
He has n't come back yet?

SECOND BLIND MAN (*who also was born blind*).
You have awakened me.

FIRST BLIND MAN.
I was sleeping, too.

THIRD BLIND MAN (*also born blind*).
I was sleeping, too.

FIRST BLIND MAN.
He has n't come yet?

SECOND BLIND MAN.
I hear nothing coming.

THIRD BLIND MAN.

It is time to go back to the Asylum.

FIRST BLIND MAN.

We ought to find out where we are.

SECOND BLIND MAN.

It has grown cold since he left.

FIRST BLIND MAN.

We ought to find out where we are!

THE VERY OLD BLIND MAN.

Does any one know where we are?

THE VERY OLD BLIND WOMAN.

We were walking a very long while; we must be a long way from the Asylum.

FIRST BLIND MAN.

Oh! the women are opposite us?

THE VERY OLD BLIND WOMAN.

We are sitting opposite you.

FIRST BLIND MAN.

Wait, I am coming over where you are. [*He rises and gropes in the dark.*] — Where are you? — Speak! let me hear where you are!

The Blind.

THE VERY OLD BLIND WOMAN.

Here; we are sitting on stones.

FIRST BLIND MAN.

[*Advances and stumbles against the fallen tree and the rocks.*] There is something between us.

SECOND BLIND MAN.

We had better keep our places.

THIRD BLIND MAN.

Where are you sitting? — Will you come over by us?

THE VERY OLD BLIND WOMAN.

We dare not rise!

THIRD BLIND MAN.

Why did he separate us?

FIRST BLIND MAN.

I hear praying on the women's side.

SECOND BLIND MAN.

Yes; the three old women are praying.

FIRST BLIND MAN.

This is no time for prayer!

SECOND BLIND MAN.

You will pray soon enough, in the dormitory!
[The three old women continue their prayers.]

THIRD BLIND MAN.

I should like to know who it is I am sitting by.

SECOND BLIND MAN.

I think I am next to you. [*They feel about them.*]

THIRD BLIND MAN.

We can't reach each other.

FIRST BLIND MAN.

Nevertheless, we are not far apart. [*He feels about him and strikes with his staff the fifth blind man, who utters a muffled groan.*] The one who cannot hear is beside us.

SECOND BLIND MAN.

I don't hear everybody; we were six just now.

FIRST BLIND MAN.

I am going to count. Let us question the women, too; we must know what to depend upon. I hear the three old women praying all the time; are they together?

THE VERY OLD BLIND WOMAN.

They are sitting beside me, on a rock.

FIRST BLIND MAN.

I am sitting on dead leaves.

THIRD BLIND MAN.

And the beautiful blind girl, where is she?

THE VERY OLD BLIND WOMAN.

She is near them that pray.

SECOND BLIND MAN.

Where is the mad woman, and her child?

THE YOUNG BLIND GIRL.

He sleeps; do not awaken him!

FIRST BLIND MAN.

Oh! how far away you are from us! I thought you were opposite me!

THIRD BLIND MAN.

We know — nearly — all we need to know. Let us chat a little, while we wait for the priest to come back.

THE VERY OLD BLIND WOMAN.

He told us to wait for him in silence.

THIRD BLIND MAN.

We are not in a church.

THE VERY OLD BLIND WOMAN.

You do not know where we are.

THIRD BLIND MAN.

I am afraid when I am not speaking.

SECOND BLIND MAN.

Do you know where the priest went?

THIRD BLIND MAN.

I think he leaves us for too long a time.

FIRST BLIND MAN.

He is getting too old. It looks as though he himself has no longer seen for some time. He will not admit it, for fear another should come to take his place among us; but I suspect he hardly sees at all any more. We must have another guide; he no longer listens to us, and we are getting too numerous. He and the three nuns are the only people in the house who can see; and they are all older than we are! — I am sure he has misled us and that he is looking for the road. Where has he gone? — He has no right to leave us here. . . .

THE VERY OLD BLIND MAN.

He has gone a long way: I think he said so to the women.

FIRST BLIND MAN.

He no longer speaks except to the women? — Do we no longer exist? — We shall have to complain of him in the end.

THE VERY OLD BLIND MAN.

To whom will you complain?

FIRST BLIND MAN.

I don't know yet; we shall see, we shall see. — But where has he gone, I say? — I am asking the women.

THE VERY OLD BLIND WOMAN.

He was weary with walking such a long time. I think he sat down a moment among us. He has been very sad and very feeble for several days. He is afraid since the physician died. He is alone. He hardly speaks any more. I don't know what has happened. He insisted on going out to-day. He said he wished to see the Island, a last time, in the sunshine, before winter came. The winter will be very long and cold, it seems, and the ice comes already from the North. He was very uneasy, too: they say the storms of the last few days have swollen the river and all the dikes are shaken. He said also that the sea frightened him; it is troubled without cause, it seems, and the coast of the Island is no longer high enough. He wished to see; but he did not tell us what he saw. — At present, I think he has gone to get some bread and water for the mad woman. He said he would have to go a long way, perhaps. We must wait.

THE YOUNG BLIND GIRL.

He took my hands when he left; and his hands shook as if he were afraid. Then he kissed me. . . . .

FIRST BLIND MAN.

Oh! oh!

THE YOUNG BLIND GIRL.

I asked him what had happened. He told me he did not know what was going to happen. He told me the reign of old men was going to end, perhaps. . . .

FIRST BLIND MAN.

What did he mean by saying that?

THE YOUNG BLIND GIRL.

I did not understand him. He told me he was going over by the great lighthouse.

FIRST BLIND MAN.

Is there a lighthouse here?

THE YOUNG BLIND GIRL.

Yes, at the north of the Island. I believe we are not far from it. He said he saw the light of the beacon even here, through the leaves. He has never seemed more sorrowful than to-day, and I believe he has been weeping for several days. I do not know why, but I wept also without seeing him. I did not hear him go away. I did not question him any further. I was aware that he smiled very gravely; I was aware that he closed his eyes and wished to be silent. . . .

FIRST BLIND MAN.

He said nothing to us of all that!

THE YOUNG BLIND GIRL.

You do not listen when he speaks!

THE VERY OLD BLIND WOMAN.

You all murmur when he speaks!

SECOND BLIND MAN.

He merely said "Good-night" to us when he went away.

THIRD BLIND MAN.

It must be very late.

FIRST BLIND MAN.

He said "Good-night" two or three times when he went away, as if he were going to sleep. I was aware that he was looking at me when he said "Good-night; good-night." — The voice has a different sound when you look at any one fixedly.

FIFTH BLIND MAN.

Pity the blind!

The Blind.   71

FIRST BLIND MAN.

Who is that, talking nonsense?

SECOND BLIND MAN.

I think it is he who is deaf.

FIRST BLIND MAN.

Be quiet! — This is no time for begging!

THIRD BLIND MAN.

Where did he go to get his bread and water?

THE VERY OLD BLIND WOMAN.

He went toward the sea.

THIRD BLIND MAN.

Nobody goes toward the sea like that at his age!

SECOND BLIND MAN.

Are we near the sea?

THE OLD BLIND WOMAN.

Yes; keep still a moment; you will hear it.
  [Murmur of a sea, near by and very calm, against the cliffs.]

SECOND BLIND MAN.

I hear only the three old women praying.

THE VERY OLD BLIND WOMAN.

Listen well; you will hear it across their prayers.

SECOND BLIND MAN.

Yes; I hear something not far from us.

THE VERY OLD BLIND MAN.

It was asleep; one would say that it awaked.

FIRST BLIND MAN.

He was wrong to bring us here; I do not like to hear that noise.

THE VERY OLD BLIND MAN.

You know quite well the Island is not large. It can be heard whenever one goes outside the Asylum close.

SECOND BLIND MAN.

I never listened to it.

THIRD BLIND MAN.

It seems close beside us to-day; I do not like to hear it so near.

SECOND BLIND MAN.

No more do I; besides, we did n't ask to go out from the Asylum.

THIRD BLIND MAN.

We have never come so far as this; it was needless to bring us so far.

The Blind.

THE VERY OLD BLIND WOMAN.

The weather was very fine this morning; he wanted to have us enjoy the last sunny days, before shutting us up all winter in the Asylum.

FIRST BLIND MAN.

But I prefer to stay in the Asylum.

THE VERY OLD BLIND WOMAN.

He said also that we ought to know something of the little Island we live on. He himself had never been all over it; there is a mountain that no one has climbed, valleys one fears to go down into, and caves into which no one has ever yet penetrated. Finally he said we must not always wait for the sun under the vaulted roof of the dormitory; he wished to lead us as far as the seashore. He has gone there alone.

THE VERY OLD BLIND MAN.

He is right. We must think of living.

FIRST BLIND MAN.

But there is nothing to see outside!

SECOND BLIND MAN.

Are we in the sun, now?

THIRD BLIND MAN.

Is the sun still shining?

SIXTH BLIND MAN.

I think not : it seems very late.

SECOND BLIND MAN.

What time is it?

THE OTHERS.

I do not know. — Nobody knows.

SECOND BLIND MAN.

Is it light still? [*To the sixth blind man.*] — Where are you? — How is it, you who can see a little, how is it?

SIXTH BLIND MAN.

I think it is very dark; when there is sunlight, I see a blue line under my eyelids. I did see one, a long while ago; but now, I no longer perceive anything.

FIRST BLIND MAN.

For my part, I know it is late when I am hungry : and I am hungry.

THIRD BLIND MAN.

Look up at the sky; perhaps you will see something there !

> [All lift their heads skyward, with the exception of the three who were born blind, who continue to look upon the ground.]

SIXTH BLIND MAN.

I do not know whether we are under the sky.

FIRST BLIND MAN.

The voice echoes as if we were in a cavern.

THE VERY OLD BLIND MAN.

I think, rather, that it echoes so because it is evening.

THE YOUNG BLIND GIRL.

It seems to me that I feel the moonlight on my hands.

THE VERY OLD BLIND WOMAN.

I believe there are stars; I hear them.

THE YOUNG BLIND GIRL.

So do I.

FIRST BLIND MAN.

I hear no noise.

SECOND BLIND MAN.

I hear only the noise of our breathing.

THE VERY OLD BLIND MAN.

I believe the women are right.

FIRST BLIND MAN.

I never heard the stars.

THE TWO OTHERS WHO WERE BORN BLIND.

Nor we, either.

[A flight of night birds alights suddenly in the foliage.]

SECOND BLIND MAN.

Listen! listen! — what is up there above us? — Do you hear?

THE VERY OLD BLIND MAN.

Something has passed between us and the sky!

SIXTH BLIND MAN.

There is something stirring over our heads; but we cannot reach there!

FIRST BLIND MAN.

I do not recognize that noise. — I should like to go back to the Asylum.

SECOND BLIND MAN.

We ought to know where we are!

SIXTH BLIND MAN.

I have tried to get up; there is nothing but thorns about me; I dare not stretch out my hands.

THIRD BLIND MAN.

We ought to know where we are!

THE VERY OLD BLIND MAN.

We cannot know!

SIXTH BLIND MAN.

We must be very far from the house. I no longer understand any of the noises.

THIRD BLIND MAN.

For a long time I have smelled the odor of dead leaves —

SIXTH BLIND MAN.

Is there any of us who has seen the Island in the past, and can tell us where we are?

THE VERY OLD BLIND WOMAN.

We were all blind when we came here.

FIRST BLIND MAN.

We have never seen.

SECOND BLIND MAN.

Let us not alarm ourselves needlessly. He will come back soon; let us wait a little longer. But in the future, we will not go out any more with him.

THE VERY OLD BLIND MAN.

We cannot go out alone.

FIRST BLIND MAN.

We will not go out at all. I had rather not go out.

SECOND BLIND MAN.

We had no desire to go out. Nobody asked him to.

THE VERY OLD BLIND WOMAN.

It was a feast-day in the Island; we always go out on the great holidays.

THIRD BLIND MAN.

He tapped me on the shoulder while I was still asleep, saying: "Rise, rise; it is time, the sun is shining!" — Is it? I had not perceived it. I never saw the sun.

THE VERY OLD BLIND MAN.

I have seen the sun, when I was very young.

THE VERY OLD BLIND WOMAN.

So have I; a very long time ago; when I was a child; but I hardly remember it any longer.

THIRD BLIND MAN.

Why does he want us to go out every time the sun shines? Who can tell the difference? I never know whether I take a walk at noon or at midnight.

SIXTH BLIND MAN.

I had rather go out at noon; I guess vaguely then at a great white light, and my eyes make great efforts to open.

THIRD BLIND MAN.

I prefer to stay in the refectory, near the sea-coal fire; there was a big fire this morning. . . .

SECOND BLIND MAN.

He could take us into the sun in the courtyard. There the walls are a shelter; you cannot go out when the gate is shut, — I always shut it. — Why are you touching my left elbow?

FIRST BLIND MAN.

I have not touched you. I can't reach you.

SECOND BLIND MAN.

I tell you somebody touched my elbow!

FIRST BLIND MAN.

It was not any of us.

SECOND BLIND MAN.

I should like to go away.

THE VERY OLD BLIND WOMAN.

My God! my God! Tell us where we are!

FIRST BLIND MAN.

We cannot wait for eternity.
[A clock, very far away, strikes twelve slowly.]

THE VERY OLD BLIND WOMAN.

Oh, how far we are from the asylum!

THE VERY OLD BLIND MAN.

It is midnight.

SECOND BLIND MAN.

It is noon. — Does any one know? — Speak!

SIXTH BLIND MAN.

I do not know, but I think we are in the dark.

FIRST BLIND MAN.

I don't know any longer where I am; we slept too long —

SECOND BLIND MAN.

I am hungry.

THE OTHERS.

We are hungry and thirsty.

SECOND BLIND MAN.

Have we been here long?

THE VERY OLD BLIND WOMAN.

It seems as if I had been here centuries!

SIXTH BLIND MAN.

I begin to understand where we are. . . .

THIRD BLIND MAN.

We ought to go toward the side where it struck midnight. . . .

[All at once the night birds scream exultingly in the darkness]

FIRST BLIND MAN.

Do you hear? — Do you hear?

SECOND BLIND MAN.

We are not alone here!

THIRD BLIND MAN.

I suspected something a long while ago: we are overheard. — Has he come back?

FIRST BLIND MAN.

I don't know what it is: it is above us.

SECOND BLIND MAN.

Did the others hear nothing? — You are always silent!

THE VERY OLD BLIND MAN.

We are listening still.

THE YOUNG BLIND GIRL.

I hear wings about me!

THE VERY OLD BLIND WOMAN.

My God! my God! Tell us where we are!

SIXTH BLIND MAN.

I begin to understand where we are. . . . The Asylum is on the other side of the great river; we crossed the old bridge. He led us to the north of the Island. We are not far from the river, and perhaps we shall hear it if we listen a moment. . . . We must go as far as the water's edge, if he does not come back. . . . There, night and day, great ships pass, and the sailors will perceive us on the banks. It is possible that we are in the wood that surrounds the lighthouse ; but I do not know the way out. . . . Will any one follow me?

FIRST BLIND MAN.

Let us remain seated ! — Let us wait, let us wait. We do not know in what direction the great river is, and there are marshes all about the Asylum. Let us wait, let us wait. . . . He will return . . . . he must return !

SIXTH BLIND MAN.

Does any one know by what route we came here? He explained it to us as he walked.

FIRST BLIND MAN.

I paid no attention to him.

SIXTH BLIND MAN.

Did any one listen to him?

THIRD BLIND MAN.

We must listen to him in the future.

SIXTH BLIND MAN.

Were any of us born on the Island?

THE VERY OLD BLIND MAN.

You know very well we came from elsewhere.

THE VERY OLD BLIND WOMAN.

We came from the other side of the sea.

FIRST BLIND MAN.

I thought I should die on the voyage.

SECOND BLIND MAN.

So did I; we came together.

THIRD BLIND MAN.

We are all three from the same parish.

FIRST BLIND MAN.

They say you can see it from here, on a clear day, — toward the north. It has no steeple.

THIRD BLIND MAN.

We came by accident.

THE VERY OLD BLIND WOMAN.

I come from another direction. . . .

SECOND BLIND MAN.

From where?

THE VERY OLD BLIND WOMAN.

I dare no longer dream of it. . . . I hardly remember any longer when I speak of it. . . . It was too long ago. . . . It was colder there than here. . . .

THE YOUNG BLIND GIRL.

I come from very far. . . .

FIRST BLIND MAN.

Well, from where?

THE YOUNG BLIND GIRL.

I could not tell you. How would you have me explain! — It is too far from here; it is beyond the sea. I come from a great country. . . . I could only make you understand by signs: and we no longer see. . . . I have wandered too long. . . . But I have seen the sunlight and the water and the fire, mountains, faces, and strange flowers. . . . There are none such on this Island; it is too gloomy and too cold. . . . I have never recognized their perfume since I saw them last. . . . And I have seen my parents and my sisters. . . . I was too young then to know where I was. . . . I still played by the seashore. . . . But oh, how I remember having seen! . . . One day I saw the snow on a mountain-top. . . I began to distinguish the unhappy . . .

FIRST BLIND MAN.

What do you mean?

THE YOUNG BLIND GIRL.

I distinguish them yet at times by their voices. . . . I have memories which are clearer when I do not think upon them. . . .

FIRST BLIND MAN.

I have no memories.

> [A flight of large migratory birds pass clamorously, above the trees.]

THE VERY OLD BLIND MAN.

Something is passing again across the sky!

SECOND BLIND MAN.

Why did you come here?

THE VERY OLD BLIND MAN.

Of whom do you ask that?

SECOND BLIND MAN.

Of our young sister.

THE YOUNG BLIND GIRL.

I was told he could cure me. He told me I would see some day; then I could leave the Island. . . .

FIRST BLIND MAN.

We all want to leave the Island!

SECOND BLIND MAN.

We shall stay here always.

THIRD BLIND MAN.

He is too old; he will not have time to cure us.

THE YOUNG BLIND GIRL.
My lids are shut, but I feel that my eyes are alive. . . .

FIRST BLIND MAN.
Mine are open.

SECOND BLIND MAN.
I sleep with my eyes open.

THIRD BLIND MAN.
Let us not talk of our eyes!

SECOND BLIND MAN.
It is not long since you came, is it?

THE VERY OLD BLIND MAN.
One evening at prayers I heard a voice on the women's side that I did not recognize; and I knew by your voice that you were very young. . . . I would have liked to see you, to hear you. . . .

FIRST BLIND MAN.
I did n't perceive anything.

SECOND BLIND MAN.
He gave us no warning.

SIXTH BLIND MAN.
They say you are beautiful as a woman who comes from very far.

THE YOUNG BLIND GIRL.

I have never seen myself.

THE VERY OLD BLIND MAN.

We have never seen each other. We ask and we reply; we live together, we are always together, but we know not what we are! . . . In vain we touch each other with both hands; the eyes learn more than the hands. . . .

SIXTH BLIND MAN.

I see your shadows sometimes, when you are in the sun.

THE VERY OLD BLIND MAN.

We have never seen the house in which we live; in vain we feel the walls and the windows; we do not know where we live! . . .

THE VERY OLD BLIND WOMAN.

They say it is an old château, very gloomy and very wretched, where no light is ever seen except in the tower where the priest has his room.

FIRST BLIND MAN.

There is no need of light for those who do not see.

SIXTH BLIND MAN.

When I tend the flock, in the neighborhood of the Asylum, the sheep return of themselves when they see at nightfall that light in the tower . . . They have never misled me.

The Blind.

THE VERY OLD BLIND MAN.

Years and years we have been together, and we have never seen each other! You would say we were forever alone! . . . To love, one must see.

THE VERY OLD BLIND WOMAN.

I dream sometimes that I see . . .

THE VERY OLD BLIND MAN.

I see only in my dreams . . .

FIRST BLIND MAN.

I do not dream, usually, except at midnight.

SECOND BLIND MAN.

Of what can one dream where the hands are motionless?

[A flurry of wind shakes the forest, and the leaves fall, thick and gloomily.]

FIFTH BLIND MAN.

Who touched my hands?

FIRST BLIND MAN.

Something is falling about us!

THE VERY OLD BLIND MAN.

That comes from above; I don't know what it is . . .

The Blind.   89

FIFTH BLIND MAN.

Who touched my hands? — I was asleep; let me sleep!

THE VERY OLD BLIND MAN.

Nobody touched your hands.

FIFTH BLIND MAN.

Who took my hands? Answer loudly; I am a little hard of hearing . . .

THE VERY OLD BLIND MAN.

We do not know ourselves.

FIFTH BLIND MAN.

Has some one come to give us warning?

FIRST BLIND MAN.

It is useless to reply; he hears nothing.

THIRD BLIND MAN.

It must be admitted, the deaf are very unfortunate.

THE VERY OLD BLIND MAN.

I am weary of staying seated.

SIXTH BLIND MAN.

I am weary of staying here.

SECOND BLIND MAN.

It seems to me we are so far from one another. . . . Let us try to get a little nearer together, — it is beginning to get cold. . . .

THIRD BLIND MAN.

I dare not rise! We had better stay where we are.

THE VERY OLD BLIND MAN.

We do not know what there may be among us.

SIXTH BLIND MAN.

I think both my hands are in blood; I would like to stand up.

THIRD BLIND MAN.

You are leaning toward me, — I hear you.

> [The blind madwoman rubs her eyes violently, groaning and turning obstinately toward the motionless priest.]

FIRST BLIND MAN.

I hear still another noise. . . .

THE VERY OLD BLIND WOMAN.

I think it is our unfortunate sister rubbing her eyes.

SECOND BLIND MAN.

She is never doing anything else; I hear her every night.

THIRD BLIND MAN.

She is mad; she never speaks.

THE VERY OLD BLIND WOMAN.

She has never spoken since she had her child. . . . She seems always to be afraid. . . .

THE VERY OLD BLIND MAN.

You are not afraid here, then?

FIRST BLIND MAN.

Who?

THE VERY OLD BLIND MAN.

All the rest of us.

THE VERY OLD BLIND WOMAN.

Yes, yes; we are afraid.

THE YOUNG BLIND GIRL.

We have been afraid for a long time.

FIRST BLIND MAN.

Why did you ask that?

THE VERY OLD BLIND MAN.

I do not know why I asked it. . . . There is something here I do not understand. . . . It seems to me I hear weeping all at once among us. . . .

FIRST BLIND MAN.

There is no need to fear; I think it is the madwoman.

THE VERY OLD BLIND MAN.

There is something else beside. . . . I am sure there is something else beside. . . . It is not that alone that makes me afraid.

THE VERY OLD BLIND WOMAN.

She always weeps when she is going to give suck to her child.

FIRST BLIND MAN.

She is the only one that weeps so.

THE VERY OLD BLIND WOMAN.

They say she sees still at times.

FIRST BLIND MAN.

You do not hear the others weep.

THE VERY OLD BLIND MAN.

To weep, one must see.

THE YOUNG BLIND GIRL.

I smell an odor of flowers about us.

FIRST BLIND MAN.

I smell only the smell of the earth.

THE YOUNG BLIND GIRL.

There are flowers, — there are flowers about us.

SECOND BLIND MAN.

I smell only the smell of the earth.

THE VERY OLD BLIND WOMAN.

I caught the perfume of flowers in the wind. . . .

THIRD BLIND MAN.

I smell only the smell of the earth.

THE VERY OLD BLIND MAN.

I believe the women are right.

SIXTH BLIND MAN.

Where are they? — I will go pluck them.

THE YOUNG BLIND GIRL.

At your right.   Rise!

> [The sixth blind man rises slowly and advances groping, and stumbling against the bushes and trees, toward the asphodels, which he breaks and crushes on his way.]

THE YOUNG BLIND GIRL.

I hear you breaking the green stalks.   Stop! stop!

FIRST BLIND MAN.

Don't worry yourselves about flowers, but think of getting home.

SIXTH BLIND MAN.

I no longer dare return on my steps.

THE YOUNG BLIND GIRL.

You need not return. — Wait. — [*She rises.*] Oh, how cold the earth is! It is going to freeze. — [*She advances without hesitation toward the strange, pale asphodels; but she is stopped, in the neighborhood of the flowers, by the uprooted tree and the fragments of rock.*] They are here. — I cannot reach them; they are on your side.

SIXTH BLIND MAN.

I believe I am plucking them.

> [He plucks the scattered flowers, gropingly, and offers them to her; the night birds fly away.]

THE YOUNG BLIND GIRL.

It seems to me I saw these flowers in the old days. . . . I no longer know their name. . . . Alas, how sickly they are, and how soft the stems are! I hardly recognize them. . . . I think it is the flower of the dead.

> [She twines the asphodels in her hair.]

THE VERY OLD BLIND MAN.

I hear the noise of your hair.

THE YOUNG BLIND GIRL.

It is the flowers.

THE VERY OLD BLIND MAN.

We shall not see you. . . .

THE YOUNG BLIND GIRL.

I shall not see myself, any more. . . . I am cold.

> [At this moment the wind rises in the forest, and the sea roars suddenly and with violence against cliffs very near.]

FIRST BLIND MAN.

It thunders!

SECOND BLIND MAN.

I think there is a storm rising.

THE VERY OLD BLIND WOMAN.

I think it is the sea.

THIRD BLIND MAN.

The sea? — Is it the sea? — But it is hardly two steps from us! — It is at our feet! I hear it all about me! — It must be something else!

THE YOUNG BLIND GIRL.

I hear the noise of breakers at my feet.

FIRST BLIND MAN.

I think it is the wind in the dead leaves.

THE VERY OLD BLIND MAN.

I think the women are right.

THIRD BLIND MAN.

It will come here!

The Blind.

FIRST BLIND MAN.

What direction does the wind come from?

SECOND BLIND MAN.

It comes from the sea.

THE VERY OLD BLIND MAN.

It always comes from the sea. The sea surrounds us on all sides. It cannot come from anywhere else. . . .

FIRST BLIND MAN.

Let us not keep on thinking of the sea!

SECOND BLIND MAN.

We must think of it. It will reach us soon.

FIRST BLIND MAN.

You do not know if it be the sea.

SECOND BLIND MAN.

I hear its surges as if I could dip both hands in them. We cannot stay here! It is perhaps all about us.

THE VERY OLD BLIND MAN.

Where would you go?

SECOND BLIND MAN.

No matter where! no matter where! I will not hear this noise of waters any longer! Let us go! Let us go!

THIRD BLIND MAN.

I think I hear something else. — Listen!
[A sound of footfalls is heard, hurried and far away, in the dead leaves.]

FIRST BLIND MAN.

There is something coming this way.

SECOND BLIND MAN.

He is coming! He is coming! He is coming back!

THIRD BLIND MAN.

He is coming with little quick steps, like a little child.

SECOND BLIND MAN.

Let us make no complaints to him to-day.

THE VERY OLD BLIND WOMAN.

I believe that is not the step of a man!
[A great dog enters in the forest, and passes in front of the blind folk. — Silence.]

FIRST BLIND MAN.

Who's there? — Who are you? — Have pity on us, we have been waiting so long! . . . [*The dog stops, and coming to the blind man, puts his fore paws on his knees.*] Oh, oh, what have you put on my knees? What is it? . . . Is it an animal? — I believe it is a dog. . . . Oh, oh, it is the dog, it is the Asylum dog! Come here, sir, come here! He comes to save us! Come here! come here, sir!

THE OTHERS.

Come here, sir! come here!

FIRST BLIND MAN.

He has come to save us! He has followed our tracks all the way! He is licking my hands as if he had just found me after centuries! He howls for joy! He is going to die for joy! Listen, listen!

THE OTHERS.

Come here! Come here!

THE VERY OLD BLIND MAN.

Perhaps he is running ahead of somebody . . .

FIRST BLIND MAN.

No, no, he is alone. — I hear nothing coming. — We need no other guide; there is none better. He will lead us wherever we want to go; he will obey us . . .

THE VERY OLD BLIND WOMAN.

I dare not follow him. . . .

THE YOUNG BLIND GIRL.

Nor I.

FIRST BLIND MAN.

Why not? His sight is better than ours.

SECOND BLIND MAN.

Don't listen to the women!

THIRD BLIND MAN.

I believe there is a change in the sky. I breathe freely. The air is pure now . . .

THE VERY OLD BLIND WOMAN.

It is the sea wind passing about us.

SIXTH BLIND MAN.

It seems to me it is getting lighter; I believe the sun is rising . . .

THE VERY OLD BLIND WOMAN.

I believe it is getting colder. . . .

FIRST BLIND MAN.

We are going to find our way again. He is dragging me! . . . he is dragging me. He is drunk with joy! — I can no longer hold him back! . . . Follow me, follow me. We are going back to the house! . . .

  [He rises, dragged by the dog, who leads him to the motionless priest, and stops.]

THE OTHERS.

Where are you? Where are you? — Where are you going? — Take care!

FIRST BLIND MAN.

Wait, wait! Do not follow me yet; I will come back . . . He is stopping. — What is the matter with him? — Oh, oh, I touched something very cold!

SECOND BLIND MAN.

What are you saying? — We can hardly hear your voice any longer.

FIRST BLIND MAN.

I have touched — I believe I am touching a face!

THIRD BLIND MAN.

What are you saying? — We hardly understand you any longer. What is the matter with you? — Where are you? — Are you already so far away?

FIRST BLIND MAN.

Oh, oh, oh! — I do not know yet what it is. — There is a dead man in the midst of us.

THE OTHERS.

A dead man in the midst of us? — Where are you? Where are you?

FIRST BLIND MAN.

There is a dead man among us, I tell you! Oh, oh, I touched a dead man's face! — You are sitting beside a dead man! One of us must have died suddenly. Why don't you speak, so that I may know who are still alive? Where are you? — Answer! answer, all of you!

> [The blind folk reply in turn, with the exception of the madwoman and the deaf man. The three old women have ceased their prayers.]

FIRST BLIND MAN.

I no longer distinguish your voices . . . You all speak alike! . . . Your voices are all trembling.

THIRD BLIND MAN.

There are two that have not answered . . . Where are they?

> [He touches with his stick the fifth blind man.]

FIFTH BLIND MAN.

Oh! oh! I was asleep; let me sleep!

SIXTH BLIND MAN.

It is not he. — Is it the madwoman?

THE VERY OLD BLIND WOMAN.

She is sitting beside me; I can hear that she is alive . . .

FIRST BLIND MAN.

I believe . . . I believe it is the priest! — He is standing up! Come, come, come!

SECOND BLIND MAN.

He is standing up?

THIRD BLIND MAN.

Then he is not dead!

THE VERY OLD BLIND MAN.

Where is he?

SIXTH BLIND MAN.

Let us go see!

[They all rise, with the exception of the madwoman and the fifth blind man, and advance, groping, toward the dead.]

SECOND BLIND MAN.

Is he here? — Is it he?

THIRD BLIND MAN.

Yes, yes, I recognize him.

FIRST BLIND MAN.

My God! my God! what will become of us?

THE VERY OLD BLIND WOMAN.

Father! father! — Is it you? Father, what has happened? — What is the matter? — Answer us! — We are all about you. Oh! oh! oh!

THE VERY OLD BLIND MAN.

Bring some water; perhaps he still lives.

The Blind.

SECOND BLIND MAN.

Let us try . . . He might perhaps be able to take us back to the Asylum . . .

THIRD BLIND MAN.

It is useless ; I no longer hear his heart. — He is cold.

FIRST BLIND MAN.

He died without speaking a word.

THIRD BLIND MAN.

He ought to have forewarned us.

SECOND BLIND MAN.

Oh ! how old he was ! . . . This is the first time I ever touched his face . . .

THIRD BLIND MAN.

[*Feeling the corpse.*]   He is taller than we.

SECOND BLIND MAN.

His eyes are wide open. He died with his hands clasped.

FIRST BLIND MAN.

It was unreasonable to die so . . .

SECOND BLIND MAN.

He is not standing up, he is sitting on a stone.

THE VERY OLD BLIND WOMAN.

My God! my God! I did not dream of such a thing! . . . such a thing! . . . He has been sick such a long time . . . He must have suffered to-day . . . Oh, oh, oh! — He never complained; he only pressed our hands . . . One does not always understand . . . One never understands! . . . Let us go pray about him; go down on your knees . . .

[The women kneel, moaning.]

FIRST BLIND MAN.

I dare not go down on my knees.

SECOND BLIND MAN.

You cannot tell what you might kneel on here.

THIRD BLIND MAN.

Was he ill? . . . He did not tell us . . .

SECOND BLIND MAN.

I heard him muttering in a low voice as he went away. I think he was speaking to our young sister. What did he say?

FIRST BLIND MAN.

She will not answer.

SECOND BLIND MAN.

Will you no longer answer us? — Where are you, I say? — Speak.

THE VERY OLD BLIND WOMAN.

You made him suffer too much; you have made him die. . . . You would not go on; you would sit down on the stones of the road to eat; you have grumbled all day . . . I heard him sigh . . . He lost heart. . . .

FIRST BLIND MAN.

Was he ill? Did you know it?

THE VERY OLD BLIND MAN.

We knew nothing . . . We never saw him. . . . When did we ever know anything behind our poor dead eyes? . . . He never complained. Now it is too late . . . I have seen three die . . . but never in this way! . . . Now it is our turn.

FIRST BLIND MAN.

It was not I that made him suffer. — I said nothing.

SECOND BLIND MAN.

No more did I. We followed him without saying anything.

THIRD BLIND MAN.

He died, going after water for the madwoman.

FIRST BLIND MAN.

What are we going to do now? Where shall we go?

THIRD BLIND MAN.

Where is the dog?

FIRST BLIND MAN.

Here; he will not go away from the dead man.

THIRD BLIND MAN.

Drag him away! Take him off, take him off!

FIRST BLIND MAN.

He will not leave the dead man.

SECOND BLIND MAN.

We cannot wait beside a dead man. We cannot die here in the dark.

THIRD BLIND MAN.

Let us remain together; let us not scatter; let us hold one another by the hand; let us all sit on this stone . . . Where are the others? . . . Come here, come, come!

THE VERY OLD BLIND MAN.

Where are you?

THIRD BLIND MAN.

Here; I am here. Are we all together? — Come nearer me. — Where are your hands? — It is very cold.

The Blind.

THE YOUNG BLIND GIRL.

Oh, how cold your hands are!

THIRD BLIND MAN.

What are you doing?

THE YOUNG BLIND GIRL.

I was putting my hands on my eyes; I thought I was going to see all at once . . .

FIRST BLIND MAN.

Who is weeping so?

THE VERY OLD BLIND WOMAN.

It is the madwoman sobbing.

FIRST BLIND MAN.

And yet she does not know the truth.

THE VERY OLD BLIND MAN.

I think we are going to die here.

THE VERY OLD BLIND WOMAN.

Perhaps some one will come . . .

THE VERY OLD BLIND MAN.

Who else would come? . . .

THE VERY OLD BLIND WOMAN.

I do not know.

FIRST BLIND MAN.

I think the nuns will come out from the Asylum . . .

THE VERY OLD BLIND WOMAN.

They do not go out after dark.

THE YOUNG BLIND GIRL.

They never go out.

SECOND BLIND MAN.

I think the men at the great lighthouse will perceive us . . .

THE VERY OLD BLIND MAN.

They never come down from their tower.

THIRD BLIND MAN.

They will see us, perhaps. . . .

THE VERY OLD BLIND WOMAN.

They look always out to sea.

THIRD BLIND MAN.

It is cold.

THE VERY OLD BLIND MAN.

Listen to the dead leaves. I believe it is freezing.

THE YOUNG BLIND GIRL.

Oh! how hard the earth is!

THIRD BLIND MAN.

I hear on my left a sound I do not understand.

THE VERY OLD BLIND MAN.

It is the sea moaning against the rocks.

THIRD BLIND MAN.

I thought it was the women.

THE VERY OLD BLIND WOMAN.

I hear the ice breaking under the surf.

FIRST BLIND MAN.

Who is shivering so? It shakes everybody on the stone.

SECOND BLIND MAN.

I can no longer open my hands.

THE VERY OLD BLIND MAN.

I hear again a sound I do not understand.

FIRST BLIND MAN.

Who is shivering so among us? It shakes the stone.

THE VERY OLD BLIND MAN.

I think it is a woman.

THE VERY OLD BLIND WOMAN.

I think the madwoman is shivering the hardest.

THIRD BLIND MAN.

We do not hear her child.

THE VERY OLD BLIND WOMAN.

I think he is still nursing.

THE VERY OLD BLIND MAN.

He is the only one who can see where we are!

FIRST BLIND MAN.

I hear the north wind.

SIXTH BLIND MAN.

I think there are no more stars; it is going to snow.

SECOND BLIND MAN.

Then we are lost!

THIRD BLIND MAN.

If any one sleeps, he must be aroused.

THE VERY OLD BLIND MAN.

Nevertheless, I am sleepy.

[A sudden gust sweeps the dead leaves around in a whirlwind.]

THE YOUNG BLIND GIRL.

Do you hear the dead leaves? — I believe some one is coming toward us.

The Blind.

SECOND BLIND MAN.

It is the wind; listen!

THIRD BLIND MAN.

No one will ever come.

THE VERY OLD BLIND MAN.

The great cold will come . . .

THE YOUNG BLIND GIRL.

I hear walking far off.

FIRST BLIND MAN.

I hear only the dead leaves.

THE YOUNG BLIND GIRL.

I hear walking far away from us.

SECOND BLIND MAN.

I hear only the north wind.

THE YOUNG BLIND GIRL.

I tell you, some one is coming toward us.

THE VERY OLD BLIND WOMAN.

I hear a sound of very slow footsteps.

THE VERY OLD BLIND MAN.

I believe the women are right.

[It begins to snow in great flakes.]

FIRST BLIND MAN.

Oh, oh! what is it falling so cold upon my hands?

SIXTH BLIND MAN.

It is snowing.

FIRST BLIND MAN.

Let us press close to one another.

THE YOUNG BLIND GIRL.

No, but listen! The sound of footsteps!

THE VERY OLD BLIND WOMAN.

For God's sake, keep still an instant.

THE YOUNG BLIND GIRL.

They come nearer! they come nearer! listen!

[Here the child of the blind madwoman begins suddenly to wail in the darkness.]

THE VERY OLD BLIND MAN.

The child is crying.

THE YOUNG BLIND GIRL.

He sees! he sees! He must see something if he cries. [*She seizes the child in her arms and advances in the direction from which the sound of footsteps seems to come. The other women follow her anxiously and surround her.*] I am going to meet him.

THE VERY OLD BLIND MAN.

Take care.

THE YOUNG BLIND GIRL.

Oh, how he cries ! — What is the matter with him ? — Don't cry. — Don't be afraid ; there is nothing to frighten you, we are here ; we are all about you. — What do you see ? — Don't be afraid at all. — Don't cry so ! — What do you see ? — Tell me, what do you see ?

THE VERY OLD BLIND WOMAN.

The sound of footsteps draws nearer and nearer : listen, listen !

THE VERY OLD BLIND MAN.

I hear the rustling of a gown against the dead leaves.

SIXTH BLIND MAN.

Is it a woman ?

THE VERY OLD BLIND MAN.

Is it a noise of footsteps ?

FIRST BLIND MAN.

Can it be perhaps the sea in the dead leaves ?

THE YOUNG BLIND GIRL.

No, no ! They are footsteps, they are footsteps, they are footsteps !

THE VERY OLD BLIND WOMAN.

We shall know soon. Listen to the dead leaves.

THE YOUNG BLIND GIRL.

I hear them, I hear them almost beside us; listen, listen! — What do you see? What do you see?

THE VERY OLD BLIND WOMAN.

Which way is he looking?

THE YOUNG BLIND GIRL.

He keeps following the sound of the steps. — Look, look! When I turn him away, he turns back to see . . . He sees, he sees, he sees! — He must see something strange!

THE VERY OLD BLIND WOMAN [*stepping forward*].

Lift him above us, so that he may see better.

THE YOUNG BLIND GIRL.

Stand back, stand back. [*She raises the child above the group of blind folk.*] — The footsteps have stopped amongst us.

THE VERY OLD BLIND WOMAN.

They are here! They are in the midst of us! . . .

THE YOUNG BLIND GIRL.

Who are you? [*Silence.*

THE VERY OLD BLIND WOMAN.

Have pity on us!

[Silence. — The child weeps more desperately.]

[CURTAIN.]

The Seven Princesses.

Persons.

THE OLD KING.
THE OLD QUEEN.
THE PRINCE.
THE SEVEN PRINCESSES.
A MESSENGER.
CHORUS OF SAILORS.

The Seven Princesses.

[A spacious hall of marble, with laurel, lavender, and lilies in porcelain vases. A flight of seven white marble steps divides the whole hall lengthwise, and seven princesses, in white gowns and with bare arms, lie sleeping on these steps, which are furnished with cushions of pale silk. A silver lamp shines on their sleep. At the back of the hall, a door with powerful bolts. To the right and left of this door large windows whose panes reach down to the level of the tiles. Behind these windows, a terrace. The sun is just setting, and through the panes a dark, marshy country is seen, with pools and forests of oaks and pines. Vertically with one of the windows, between huge willows, a gloomy canal without a bend, on the horizon of which a large man-of-war approaches.
The old King, the old Queen and the Messenger come forward upon the terrace and watch the approach of the man-of-war.]

THE QUEEN.

It comes with all sails set. . . .

THE KING.

I do not see it well through the fog. . . .

The Seven Princesses.

QUEEN.

They are rowing — they are all rowing. . . . I believe they are going to come to the very windows of the château. . . . You would say it had a thousand feet . . . the sails touch the branches of the willows. . . .

KING.

It looks larger than the canal. . . .

QUEEN.

They are stopping. . . .

KING.

I do not know how they will be able to go back. . . .

QUEEN.

They are stopping . . . they are stopping. They are coming to anchor. . . . They are making fast to the willows. . . . Oh! oh! I believe the prince is coming down — . . .

KING.

Just look at the swans. . . . They are going to meet him. . . . They are going to see what it is. . . .

QUEEN.

Are they still asleep?

[They come and look through the windows into the hall.]

The Seven Princesses.

KING.

Let us wake them. . . . I told you so a long while ago; they must be wakened. . . .

QUEEN.

Let us wait till he come. . . . It is too late now. . . . He is here; he is here! — My God, my God! what shall we do? — I dare not! I dare not! . . . They are too ill. . . .

KING.

Shall I open the door?

QUEEN.

No, no! Wait! Let us wait! — Oh, how they sleep! how they still sleep! . . . They do not know he has come back — they do not know he is here. . . . I dare not wake them . . . the physician forbade it . . . let us not wake them. . . . Let us not wake them yet. . . . Oh, oh! I hear a sound of footsteps on the bridge. . . .

KING.

He is here! He is here! . . . He is at the foot of the terrace! . . .

[*They leave the window.*

QUEEN.

Where is he? Where is he? — Is it he? — I should no longer know him! . . . Yes, yes; I should know him still! Oh, how tall he is!

how tall he is! He is at the foot of the steps! . . . Marcellus! Marcellus! Is it you? Is it you? — Come up! come up! We are so old — we can no longer come down to you. . . . Come up! come up! come up!

KING.

Take care you do not fall! . . . the steps are very old . . . they all shake. . . . Take care! . . .

QUEEN.

Come up! come up! come up!

[The Prince ascends to the terrace and throws himself in the arms of the King and Queen.]

THE PRINCE.

My poor grandam! My poor grandfather!

[*They kiss.*

QUEEN.

Oh, how handsome you are! — How you have grown, my child! — How tall you are, my little Marcellus! — I do not see you well; my eyes are full of tears. . . .

PRINCE.

Oh, my poor grandam, how white your hair is! . . . Oh, my poor grandfather, how white your beard is! . . .

KING.

We are poor little old people; our turn is coming. . . .

The Seven Princesses.

PRINCE.

Grandfather, grandfather, why do you bend so?

KING.

I am always bent. . . .

QUEEN.

We have waited for you so long! . . .

PRINCE.

Oh, my poor grandam, how you tremble this evening! . . .

QUEEN.

I always tremble so, my child. . . .

PRINCE.

Oh, my poor grandfather! Oh, my poor grandam! I hardly know you any longer. . . .

KING.

No more do I! no more do I! I no longer see very well. . . .

QUEEN.

Where have you been so long, my child? — Oh, how tall you are! — You are taller than we! . . . There, there, I am weeping as if you were dead!

PRINCE.

Why do you receive me with tears in your eyes?

QUEEN.

No, no, it is not tears, my child. . . . It is not the same thing as tears. . . . Nothing has happened. . . . Nothing has happened. . . .

PRINCE.

Where are my seven cousins?

QUEEN.

Here, here; listen, listen. . . . do not speak too loud; they sleep still; we must not speak of those who sleep . . .

PRINCE.

They sleep? . . . Are they still living, — all seven? . . .

QUEEN.

Yes, yes, yes; take care, take care. . . . They are asleep here; they are always asleep. . . .

PRINCE.

They are always asleep? . . . What? what? what? — Do they —? . . . all seven! all seven! . . .

QUEEN.

Oh, oh, oh! what did you think? . . . what did you dare think, Marcellus, Marcellus? Take care! — They are here; come, look through the window . . . come, look. . . . Quick, quick; come quick! It is time to see them. . . .

[They draw near the windows and look into the hall. A long silence.]

The Seven Princesses.

PRINCE.

It is my seven cousins? . . . I do not see plainly. . . .

QUEEN.

Yes, yes; they are all seven there on the steps. . . . Do you see them? Do you see them?

PRINCE.

I see only some white shadows. . . .

QUEEN.

It is your seven cousins! . . . Do you see them in the mirrors? . . .

PRINCE.

It is my seven cousins? . . .

QUEEN.

Pray, look in the mirrors at the very end of the hall . . . you will see them; you will see them. . . . Come here, come here; you will see better, perhaps.

PRINCE.

I see! I see! I see! I see them, — all seven! . . . One, two, three [*he hesitates a moment*], four, five, six, seven. . . . I hardly recognize them. . . . I do not recognize them at all. . . . Oh, how white they are, all seven! . . . Oh, how fair they are, all seven! . . . Oh, how pale they are, all seven! . . . But why do all the seven sleep?

The Seven Princesses.

QUEEN.

They always sleep. . . . They have slept here since noon. . . . They are so ill! . . . You can no longer wake them. . . . They did not know you were about to come. . . . We have not dared wake them. . . . We must wait. . . . They must awake of themselves. . . . They are not happy; it is not our fault. . . . We are too old, too old; everybody is too old for them. . . . People are too old without knowing it. . . .

PRINCE.

Oh, how beautiful they are! how beautiful they are! . . .

QUEEN.

They hardly live any longer since they have been here; — they have been here ever since their parents died. . . . It is too cold in this château. . . . They come from the warm countries. . . . They are alway seeking the sunshine; but there is almost none. . . . There was a little on the canal this morning; but the trees are too tall; there is too much shade; there is nothing but shade. . . . There are too many fogs, and the sky is never clear. . . . — Oh, how you look at them! — Do you see anything extraordinary?

PRINCE.

Oh, how pale they are, all seven!

QUEEN.

They are still fasting. . . . They could not stay in the garden any longer; the lawn dazzled them. . . . They have the fever. . . . They returned this noon holding one another by the hand. . . . They are so weak they can hardly walk alone now. . . . They shook with fever, — all seven. And no one knows what ails them. . . . They sleep here every day.

PRINCE.

They are strange. . . . Oh, oh, they are strange! . . . I dare no longer look at them. Is this their bedchamber?

QUEEN.

No, no; it is not their bedchamber. . . . You see plainly; there are no beds. Their seven little beds are above, — in the tower. . . . They are here, waiting for the night.

PRINCE.

I begin to make them out. . . .

QUEEN.

Draw near, draw near; but do not touch the windows. . . . You will see better when the sun has set; it is too light still outside. . . . You will see better soon. Stand close to the window-panes; but make no noise. . . .

PRINCE.

Oh, how light it is in the hall! . . .

QUEEN.

It will be lighter still when the night has come. . . . It is about to fall. . . .

KING.

What is that about to fall?

QUEEN.

I spoke of the night. — Do you see anything?

PRINCE.

There is a great crystal vase upon a tripod. . . .

QUEEN.

That is nothing; it is water; they are so thirsty when they wake! . . .

PRINCE.

But why is that lamp burning?

QUEEN.

They always light it. They knew they would sleep a long time. They lighted it this noon that they might not wake in the darkness. . . . They are afraid of the dark. . . .

PRINCE.

They have grown tall!

The Seven Princesses.

QUEEN.

They are growing yet. . . . They are getting too tall. . . . It is perhaps that which makes them so ill. . . . Do you recognize them?

PRINCE.

I should recognize them, perhaps, if I saw them in broad daylight. . . .

QUEEN.

You have played so often with them when they were little. . . . Open your eyes. . . .

PRINCE.

I see plainly only their little bare feet. . . .

KING.

[*Looking in at another window.*] I cannot see in very clearly this evening. . . .

PRINCE.

They are too far from us. . . .

QUEEN.

There is something over the mirrors this evening; I do not see quite what it is. . . .

PRINCE.

There is a mist over the window-panes. . . . I am going to see if I can wipe it away. . . .

QUEEN.

No, no! do not touch the window! They would wake with a start! — It is on the inside; it is on the other side; it is the heat of the hall. . . .

PRINCE.

Six of them I can make out very well; but there is one in the middle. . . .

KING.

They all look alike; I only distinguish them by their necklaces of precious stones. . . .

PRINCE.

There is one I cannot see well. . . .

QUEEN.

Which do you like best?

PRINCE.

The one you cannot see well. . . .

QUEEN.

Which? I am a little hard of hearing. . . .

PRINCE.

The one you cannot see well. . . .

KING.

Which one is it you cannot see well? I hardly see any of them.

The Seven Princesses.

PRINCE.

The one in the middle. . . .

QUEEN.

I knew well you would see her only! . . .

PRINCE.

Who is it?

QUEEN.

You know well who it is; I need not tell you.

PRINCE.

It is Ursula?

QUEEN.

Why, yes; why, yes; why, yes! You know well it is Ursula! it is Ursula! It is Ursula, who has waited for you for seven years! all night long! all night long! all day long! all day long! . . . Do you recognize her? . . .

PRINCE.

I do not see her well; there is a shadow over her. . . .

QUEEN.

Yes, there is a shadow over her; I do not know what it is. . . .

PRINCE.

I think it is the shadow of a column. . . . I shall see her better soon, when the sun has wholly set. . . .

QUEEN.

No, no; it is no shadow of the sun. . . .

PRINCE.

We shall see if the shadow moves away. . . .

KING.

I see what it is; it is the shadow of the lamp.

QUEEN.

She is lying differently from the others. . . .

KING.

She sleeps more soundly, that is all. . . .

PRINCE.

She sleeps like a little child. . . .

KING.

Come to this window; you will see better, perhaps.

PRINCE.

[*Going to another window.*] I see her no better. It is the face I cannot see. . . .

QUEEN.

Come to this window; you will see better perhaps. . . .

PRINCE.

[*Going to another window.*] I see her no better. . . . It is very difficult to see her. . . . One would say she was hiding. . . .

QUEEN.

The face is almost invisible. . . .

PRINCE.

I see the body very well, but I do not make out the face. . . . I think it is entirely turned heavenward. . . .

QUEEN.

But you look only at one ! . . .

PRINCE.

[*Still looking.*] She is taller than the others. . . .

QUEEN.

But do not look always at the only one we cannot see. . . . There are six others ! . . .

PRINCE.

I look at them, too. . . . Oh, how clearly one can see the others ! . . .

QUEEN.

Do you recognize them ? — There is Geneviève, — Helen, — and Christabel . . . and on the other side there is Magdalen, — Clara, — and Claribel with the emeralds. . . . — Just see; I believe they are holding each other, all seven, by the hand. . . . They fell asleep, taking hold of hands. . . . Oh, oh ! the little sisters ! . . . You would say they were afraid of losing each other in their sleep. . . . My God, my God ! I wish they would awake ! . . .

PRINCE.

Yes, yes; let us wake them. . . . Will you let me wake them? . . .

QUEEN.

No, no; not yet, not yet. . . . Let us not look at them any more; come, do not look at them any more; they will suddenly have bad dreams. . . . I will look at them no more; I will look at them no more. . . . I might break the glass! . . . Let us not look at them any more, we should be frightened! . . . Come away, come away, to the foot of the terrace; we will talk of other things; we have so many things to say. . . . Come away, come away; they will be afraid if they turn over; they will be afraid if they see us at all the windows. [*To the old* KING.] You too, you too; come away, do not glue your white beard to the panes so . . . you do not know how terrifying you are! . . . — For the love of God, do not stay, both of you, at the windows! . . . Oh, come away; come away, I tell you! . . . You do not know what is going to happen. . . . Come here, come here, turn away, turn away! Look the other way! Look the other way a moment! . . . They are ill, they are ill! . . . Let us go further away. . . . Let them sleep alone! . . .

PRINCE.

[*Turning.*] What is the matter? — Why, what is the matter? — Oh, how dark it is without! . . . Where are you? I cannot find you. . . .

The Seven Princesses.

KING.

Wait a moment; you have the light of the hall in your eyes still. . . . I do not see either. . . . Come. We are here. . . .

[They leave the windows.

PRINCE.

Oh, how dark it is in the fields! . . . Where are we?

KING.

The sun has set. . . .

QUEEN.

Marcellus; why did you not come sooner, Marcellus?

PRINCE.

The messenger has told you; I have thought only of coming. . . .

QUEEN.

They have waited for you so many years! They have been always in this marble hall; they have watched the canal day and night. . . . On sunny days they have gone on the other bank . . . there is a hill there, from which you can see further; you cannot see the sea; but you can see the rocks. . . .

PRINCE.

What is that gleam under the trees?

KING.

It is the canal by which you came; there is always a gleam on the water. . . .

PRINCE.

Oh, how dark it is to-night! — I no longer know where I am; I am like a stranger here. . . .

KING.

The sky is overcast suddenly. . . .

PRINCE.

There is a breeze in the willows. . . .

KING.

There is a breeze day and night in the willows; we are not far from the sea. — Listen; it rains already. . . .

PRINCE.

One would say there was weeping about the château. . . .

KING.

It is the rain falling on the water; it is a very gentle rain. . . .

QUEEN.

One would say there was weeping in the sky. . . .

PRINCE.

Oh, how the water sleeps between the walls! . . .

QUEEN.

It always sleeps so; it is very old too. . . .

PRINCE.

The swans have sought shelter under the bridge. . . .

KING.

And here are peasants bringing home their flocks. . . .

PRINCE.

They seem to me very old and very poor. . . .

KING.

They are very poor; I am king of very poor people. . . . It is beginning to grow cold. . . .

PRINCE.

What is there yonder, across the water?

KING.

Down there? — It was some flowers; the cold has killed them. . . .

> [At this moment, far off across the fields a monotonous song is heard, of which the refrain only can be distinguished, taken up in chorus at regular intervals.]

FAR-AWAY VOICES.

The Atlantic! The Atlantic!

KING.

What is that?

PRINCE.

It is the sailors; — I think they are turning the ship; they are preparing to depart. . . .

FAR-AWAY VOICES.

We shall return no more! We shall return no more!

QUEEN.

Already all its sails are set. . . .

PRINCE.

They depart to-night. . . .

FAR-AWAY VOICES.

The Atlantic! The Atlantic!

KING.

Is it true that they will return no more?

PRINCE.

I do not know; perhaps it will not be the same ones. . . .

FAR-AWAY VOICES.

We shall return no more! We shall return no more!

QUEEN.

You do not look happy, my child.

PRINCE.

I? — Why should I not be happy? — I came to see her, and I have seen her . . . I can see her nearer if I will . . . I can sit by her side if I will. . . . Can I not open the doors and take her hand? I may kiss her when I will; I have only to wake her. Why should I be unhappy?

QUEEN.

You do not look happy, though! . . . I am nearly seventy-five years old now . . . and I have been waiting for you always! . . . It is not you, not you! . . . It is no longer you! . . .

[She turns away her head and sobs.]

KING.

What is the matter? Why, what is the matter? Why do you weep all at once?

QUEEN.

It is nothing; it is nothing; — it is not I who weep. . . . Do not mind me; — one weeps often without reason; — I am so old to-day. — It is over. . . .

PRINCE.

I shall look happier soon. . . .

QUEEN.

Come, come; they are perhaps there with open eyes. . . . Give me your hand; lead me to the windows; let us go look in at the windows. . . .

FAR-AWAY VOICES.

The Atlantic! The Atlantic!
[They all return and look through the windows.]

PRINCE.

I cannot see yet. . . . It is too light. . . .

QUEEN.

There is something changed in the hall! . . .

KING.

I see nothing at all.

PRINCE.

It is brighter than before. . . .

QUEEN.

It is not the same; there is something changed in the hall. . . .

PRINCE.

My eyes are not yet used to the light. . . .

QUEEN.

They are no longer all in the same position! . . .

PRINCE.

Yes, yes; I believe they have made a little movement. . . .

The Seven Princesses.

QUEEN.

Oh, oh! Christabel and Claribel? . . . See, see! . . . They were holding Ursula by the hand. . . . They no longer hold their sister by the hand. . . . They have let go her hands. . . . They have turned the other way. . . .

PRINCE.

They were on the point of waking. . . .

QUEEN.

We have come too late! We have come too late! . . .

KING.

I see only the lilies by the windows: — they are closed. . . .

PRINCE.

They know it is nightfall. . . .

KING.

And yet there is a light there. . . .

PRINCE.

She is holding one of her hands strangely. . . .

QUEEN.

Who is?

PRINCE.

Ursula. . . .

QUEEN.

What is that hand? . . . I did not see it just now. . . .

PRINCE.

The others concealed it. . . .

KING.

I do not know what you mean; I do not even see the mirrors. . . .

QUEEN.

She will be hurt! . . . She will be hurt! . . . She cannot sleep so; it is not natural . . . I wish she would put down her hand a little. — My God, my God, grant that she put down that little hand! . . . Her little arm must ache there so long! . . .

PRINCE.

I see nothing to sustain it . . .

QUEEN.

I cannot see her sleep so . . . I never yet saw her sleep so. . . . It is not a good sign. . . . It is not a good sign! . . . She will never be able to move her hand again. . . .

KING.

There is no reason to be so disturbed. . . .

PRINCE.

The others sleep more simply. . . .

The Seven Princesses.

QUEEN.

How tight their eyes are shut! How tight their eyes are shut! ... Oh, oh! the little sisters! the little sisters! ... What shall we do? — Oh, what shall we do about it? ...

KING.

Take care, do not speak so close to the windows. ...

QUEEN.

I am not so close as you think. ...

KING.

Your mouth is on the panes. ...

PRINCE.

I see something else — something very indistinct. ...

QUEEN.

So do I, so do I. There is something I am beginning to see. ... It stretches out to the door. ...

PRINCE.

There is something on the marble slabs. ... It is not a shadow. ... It cannot be a shadow. ... I cannot be clear what it is. ... It might be her hair. ...

QUEEN.

But why has she not bound up her hair? ... All the others have bound up their hair. ... Look. ...

PRINCE.

I tell you it is her hair! ... It stirs. ... Oh, her hair is beautiful! ... It is not the hair of a sick woman. ...

QUEEN.

She does not arrange it so for sleeping. ... You would say she had intended to go out.

PRINCE.

She said nothing to you? ...

QUEEN.

She said this noon as she closed the door: "Above all, do not wake us." — Then I kissed her, not to see that she was sad. ...

PRINCE.

They will be cold with their little feet almost naked on the marble!

QUEEN.

Yes, yes; they will be cold! — Oh, do not look so eagerly! [*To the* KING.] Nor you either! Nor you either! — Do not look every moment! Do not look all the time! — Let us not all look together! ... They are not happy! They are not happy! ...

KING.

What is it now, all at once? — Are you the only one that may see, pray? — Why, what is the matter with you this evening? — You are not reasonable any more . . . I do not understand you . . . Everybody else must look the other way; everybody else must shut their eyes. . . . But this concerns us as much as you, I think. . . .

QUEEN.

Oh, I know it concerns you. . . . Do not speak so, for the love of God! . . . Oh, oh! . . . Do not look at me! Do not look at me just now! . . . My God, my God! how motionless they are! . . .

KING.

They will not wake to-night; we would do better to go and sleep too. . . .

QUEEN.

Let us wait still; let us wait still. . . . We shall see perhaps what it is. . . .

KING.

We cannot look forever through the window-panes; something must be done. . . .

PRINCE.

Perhaps we could wake them from here. . . .

KING.

I am going to knock softly on the door.

QUEEN.

No, no! Never! Never! . . . Oh! No, not you, not you! You would knock too loud. . . . Take care! Oh, take care! They are afraid of everything . . . I will knock myself on the window, if it must be. . . . They must see who knocks. . . . Wait, wait. . . .

[*She knocks very softly at the window.*

PRINCE.

They do not wake. . . .

KING.

I see nothing at all. . . .

QUEEN.

I am going to knock a little louder. . . . [*She knocks again at the window.*] They do not stir yet . . . [*The* QUEEN *knocks again at the window.*] — You would say the hall was full of cotton . . . — Are you sure this is sleep? — Perhaps they have fainted . . . I cannot see them breathe . . . [*The* QUEEN *knocks again at another window*]: Knock a little harder . . . Knock on the other panes! Oh, oh! these little panes are thick! [*The* QUEEN *and the* PRINCE *knock anxiously with both hands.*] How motionless they are! How motionless they are! — It is the heavy sleep of the sick . . . It is the sleep of fever, which will not go away . . . I want to see them near! . . . They do not hear the noise we make. . . . It is not a natural sleep. . . . It is not a healthy sleep . . . I dare not knock harder. . . .

PRINCE.

[*Listening against the panes.*] I do not hear the least noise. . . .

[A long silence.

QUEEN.

[*Her face against the panes and in a sudden burst of tears.*] Oh, how they sleep! how they sleep! . . . My God, my God! deliver them, deliver them! — How their little hearts sleep! — You cannot hear their little hearts! — It is a fearful sleep! — Oh, oh! how fearful people are, asleep! . . . I am always afraid in their sleeping-room! . . . I no longer see their little souls! . . . Where then are their little souls! . . . They make me afraid! they make me afraid! — It is now that I see it! . . . How they sleep, the little sisters! Oh, how they sleep, how they sleep! . . . I believe they will sleep forever! . . . My God, my God, I pity them! . . . They are not happy! they are not happy! . . . Now I see it all! . . . Seven little souls all night! . . . Seven little helpless souls! . . . Seven little friendless souls! . . . Their mouths are wide open. . . . Seven little open mouths! . . . Oh, I am sure they are thirsty! . . . I am sure they are terribly thirsty! . . . And all their eyes shut! . . . Oh, how alone

they are; all seven! all seven! all seven!...
And how they sleep! How they sleep!—
How they sleep, the little queens!... I am
sure they do not sleep!... Oh, what a sleep!
what a deep sleep!... Oh, wake the dear
hearts! Wake the little queens!... Wake
the little sisters! All the seven! all the seven!
... I cannot bear to see them so any longer!
My God, my God, I pity them! I pity them!
And I dare not wake them!... Oh, the light
is so faint!... so faint!... so faint...
And I dare not wake them!... [*She sobs
desperately against the window.*]

KING.

What is the matter?—What is the matter
now?—Come, come, look no longer; it is
better not to see them.... Come, come,
come. [*He tries to take her away.*

PRINCE.

Grandmother! grandmother!... What
have you seen? what have you seen?—I
have seen nothing.... There is nothing,
there is nothing....

KING.

[*To the* PRINCE.] It is nothing, it is nothing; do not mind her; it is old age, it is the
night.... She is unnerved.—Women must
weep. She weeps often in the night. [*To the*
QUEEN.] Come, come, come here.... You

will fall! — Take care. . . . Lean on me. . . . Do not weep any more; do not weep any more, come. . . . [*He kisses her tenderly.*] It is nothing; they are sleeping. . . . We sleep, too. . . . We all sleep so. . . . Have you never seen any one sleep?

QUEEN.

Never! Never as to-night! — Open the door! Open the door! . . . No one loves them enough! . . . No one can love them! — Open the door! Open the door! . . .

KING.

Yes; yes; we will open the door. . . . Be calm, be calm, — think no more of it; we will open it, we will open it. I ask nothing better; I told you to open it, just now, and you would not. . . . Now, now, do not weep any more. . . . Be reasonable. . . . I am old too, but I am reasonable. Now, now, do not weep any more. . . .

QUEEN.

There, there; it is over; I will weep no more, I will weep no more. . . . They must not hear me weeping when they wake. . . .

KING.

Come, come, I shall open the door very softly; we will go in together. . . . [*He tries to open the door; the lock grates, and, inside the hall, the latch can be seen to lift and fall back again.*]

Oh, oh! what is the matter with the lock, I wonder? — I cannot open the door . . . push a little. . . . I do not know what it can be. . . . I did not know it was so hard to get into this hall. . . . Will you try? [*The* QUEEN *tries in her turn, without success.*] It does not open. . . . I believe they have drawn the bolts. . . . Yes, yes; the door is locked; it will not open. . . .

QUEEN.

They always lock it. . . . Oh, oh! do not abandon them so! . . . They have slept so long!

PRINCE.

We might open a window. . . .

KING.

The windows do not open.

PRINCE.

It seems to me it is not so light in the hall. . . .

KING.

It is just as light there; but the sky is clearing. — Do you see the stars?

PRINCE.

What shall we do?

KING.

I do not know. . . . — There is another entrance. . . .

The Seven Princesses.   153

PRINCE.

There is another entrance?

QUEEN.

No! no! I know what you mean! . . . Not that way! not that way! I will not go down! . . .

KING.

We will not go down; we will stay here; Marcellus will go alone. . . .

QUEEN.

Oh, no, no, no! . . . Let us wait. . . .

KING.

But, after all, what will you have us do?— There is no other way to get into the hall . . . that is as clear as possible. . . .

PRINCE.

There is another entrance?

KING.

Yes; there is still a little entrance . . . you cannot see it from here . . . but you will easily find it. You must go down underneath. . . .

PRINCE.

Where must I go down?

KING.

Come here. [*He draws him a little aside.*] It is not a door . . . you could not call it a door . . . it is a trap, rather . . . it is a movable slab in the floor. It is quite at the back of the hall. . . . You must go through the vaults . . . you understand. . . . Then come up again. . . . You will need a lamp . . . you might lose yourself . . . you might dash yourself against the . . . the marble . . . do you understand? . . . Take care; there are chains between the . . . the little passages. . . . But you should know the way. . . . You went down there more than once formerly. . . .

PRINCE.

I went down there more than once formerly?

KING.

Why, yes; why, yes; where your mother . . .

PRINCE.

Where my mother . . . ? — Ah, is it there I must go? . . .

KING.

[*Makes a sign with his head.*] It is there. —. And where your father also . . .

PRINCE.

Yes, yes; I remember . . . and where others also . . .

KING.

You understand! . . . The stone is not cemented; you have only to push a little. . . . But be careful. . . . There are some slabs that are not regular. . . . Be on your guard for a bust that bends its head a little across the path . . . it is marble. . . . There is a cross, too, with arms a little long . . . be on your guard . . . do not hurry; you have plenty of time. . . .

PRINCE.

And it is there I must go? . . .

KING.

It is there! . . . He must have a lamp. [*He goes to the edge of the terrace and calls.*] A lamp! a lamp! a little lamp! . . . [*To the* PRINCE.] We will wait here at the windows. . . . We are too old to go down there. . . . We could not climb up again. . . . [*A lighted lamp is brought.*] Ah, ah, here is the lamp; take the little lamp. . . .

PRINCE.

Yes, yes; the little lamp. . . .

> [At this moment great cries of joy from the sailors are heard suddenly without. The masts, yards, and sails of the ship are illuminated, in the midst of the darkness, on the horizon of the canal, among the willows.]

KING.

Oh, oh, what is that?

PRINCE.

It is the sailors. . . . They are dancing on the bridge; they are tipsy. . . .

KING.

They have lighted up the ship. . . .

PRINCE.

It is the joy of departure. . . . They are just leaving. . . .

KING.

Well, will you go down? . . . It is this way.

QUEEN.

No, no, do not go there! . . . Do not go that way! . . . do not wake them! do not wake them! . . . You know they must have rest! . . . I am afraid! . . .

PRINCE.

I will not wake the others, if you wish. . . . I will wake one only. . . .

QUEEN.

Oh! oh! oh!

KING.

Make no noise as you enter. . . .

PRINCE.

I am afraid they will not recognize me. . .

The Seven Princesses.   157

KING.

There is no danger. . . . Eh, eh! take care of the little lamp! . . . Don't you see there is a wind? . . . the wind will blow it out! . . .

PRINCE.

I fear they will not all wake at once.

KING.

What does that matter? . . . Do not wake them roughly, that is all.

PRINCE.

I shall be all alone before them. . . . I shall look as if . . . they will be afraid. . . .

KING.

You will only wake them after putting the stone back in its place. . . . They will not notice anything. . . . They do not know what there is under the hall where they sleep. . . .

PRINCE.

They will take me for a stranger. . . .

KING.

We will be at the windows. — Go down; go down. — Take care of the lamp. — Above all, do not lose yourself in the vaults; they are of a great depth. . . . Be careful to put the slab back. . . . Come up as soon as possible. . . . We will wait at the windows. . . . Go down, go down; — careful! careful! . . .

> [The Prince leaves the terrace; the old King and the old Queen look through the windows, with their faces against the panes. — A long silence.]

FAR-AWAY VOICES.

The Atlantic! The Atlantic!

KING.

[*Turning his head and looking toward the canal.*] Ah, ah! they are going. . . . They will have a fair wind to-night. . . .

FAR-AWAY VOICES.

We shall return no more! We shall return no more!

KING.

[*Looking toward the canal.*] They will be on the open sea before midnight. . . .

VOICES.

[*Farther and farther away.*] The Atlantic! The Atlantic!

KING.

[*Looking into the hall.*] If only he does not lose himself in the darkness. . . .

VOICES.

[*Almost inaudible.*] We shall return no more! We shall return no more!
 [A silence; the ship disappears among the willows.]

KING.

[*Looking toward the canal.*] You cannot see them any longer. — [*Looking into the hall.*] He has not come yet? — [*Looking toward the canal.*] — The ship is no longer there! — [*To the* QUEEN.] — You pay no attention? — You do not answer? — Where are you? Look at the canal. — They have gone; they will be on the open sea before midnight. . . .

QUEEN.

[*Distractedly.*] They will be on the open sea before midnight. . . .

KING.

[*Looking into the hall.*] Can you see the slab he should lift? — It is covered with inscriptions; — it must be hidden by the laurels. — He has grown tall, Marcellus, has he not? — We would have done better to wake them before he landed. — I told you so. — We should have avoided all these scenes. — I do not know why he did not look happy this evening. — They were wrong to draw the bolts; I will have them taken off. — If only his lamp does not go out! — Where are you? — Do you see anything? — Why do you not answer? — If only he does not lose himself in the darkness! — Are you listening to me?

QUEEN.

If only he does not lose himself in the darkness! . . .

KING.

You are right. — Do you not find it is beginning to grow cold? — They will be cold on the marble. — It seems to me he is taking his time. — If only his little lamp does not go out! — Why do you not answer? What are you dreaming about?

QUEEN.

If only his little lamp . . . ! The stone! the stone! the stone! . . .

KING.

Is he there? — Is he coming in? — I cannot see that far. . . .

QUEEN.

It rises! it rises! . . . There is a light! . . . look . . . listen! listen! — It creaks on its hinges! . . .

KING.

I told him to go in very softly. . . .

QUEEN.

Oh, he is coming in very softly. . . . See, see, he is putting his hand through with the lamp. . . .

The Seven Princesses.

KING.

Yes, yes; I see the little lamp. . . . Why does he not enter at once? . . .

QUEEN.

He cannot. . . . He is lifting the stone very slowly. . . . Yes, yes; very slowly . . . Oh, how it creaks! how it creaks! how it creaks! . . . They will wake with a start!

KING.

I cannot see very well what is going on . . . I know the stone is very heavy. . . .

QUEEN.

He enters . . . He comes up . . . He comes up more and more slowly . . . Oh, but the stone cries now! . . . oh, oh! it cries! it cries! It wails like a child! . . . He is half in the hall! . . . Three steps more! three steps more! [*Clapping her hands.*] He is in the hall! He is in the hall! . . . Look! look! . . . They wake! . . . They all wake with a start! . . .

KING.

Has he let the slab fall?

[The Prince, letting go the sepulchral slab he has just lifted, stops, lamp in hand, at the foot of the marble steps. Six of the princesses, at the last grating of the hinges, open their eyes, stir a moment on the edge of sleep, and then rise simultaneously at his approach, their arms raised in slow attitudes of waking. One only, Ursula, remains stretched on her back on the marble steps, motionless, in the midst of her sisters, who exchange with the Prince a long look full of marvellings, bewilderments and silences.]

QUEEN.

[*At the windows.*] Ursula! Ursula! Ursula! ... She does not wake! ...

KING.

Patience! patience! — She sleeps a little heavily. ...

QUEEN.

[*Crying out, her face against the windows.*] Ursula! Ursula! — Wake her! [*Knocking on the windows.*] Marcellus! Marcellus! — Wake her! Wake her too! Ursula! Ursula! ... Marcellus! Marcellus! ... She has not heard! ... Ursula! Ursula! Arise! He is there! He is there! ... It is time! It is time! — [*Knocking at another window.*] Marcellus! Marcellus! Look before you! look! She is sleeping still! ... [*Knocking at another window.*] — Oh, oh! — Christabel! Christabel! Claribel! Claribel! ... Clara! Clara! Oh, Clara! ... She has not heard! ... [*Knocking constantly and violently on the windows.*] Ursula! Ursula! He has come back! He is there! He is there! ... It is time! It is time! ...

KING.

[*Also knocking at the windows.*] Yes; yes; wake her!... Oh, wake her!... We are waiting....

> [The Prince, unheeding the noises outside, approaches in silence the one who has not risen. He gazes upon her a moment, hesitates, bends his knee and touches one of the arms lying bare and inert on the silken cushions. At the contact of the flesh he rises suddenly, with a long and sweeping look of terror at the six princesses, who remain mute and are extremely pale. They, at first undecided and trembling with the desire to flee, stoop finally with a unanimous movement over their prostrate sister, lift her, and, in the deepest silence, bear the body, already rigid, with head dishevelled and stiff, to the highest of the seven marble steps; while the Queen, the King, and the people of the château, who have hurried to the scene, knock and cry out violently at all the windows of the hall: these two scenes take place simultaneously.]

QUEEN.

She is not asleep! She is not asleep! — It is not sleep! It is not sleep! It is no longer sleep! [*She runs desperately from window to window; she knocks at them, she shakes the iron bars; she stamps and her white unknotted hair is seen quivering against the panes.*] She is no longer sleeping, I tell you! [*To the* KING.] Oh! oh! oh! you are a man of stone!... Cry out! cry out! cry out! For God's sake! cry out, I tell you! I scream myself to death and he does not understand! — Run! run! cry! cry! He has seen nothing! nothing! nothing! nothing! never! never! never! . . .

KING.

What? what? What is it? What is it? Where must I cry out?

QUEEN.

Down there! down there! Everywhere! everywhere! on the terrace! over the water! over the meadows! . . . Cry! cry! cry! . . .

KING.

[*On the edge of the terrace.*] Oh! . . . oh! . . . Hurry! hurry! here! here! . . . Ursula! Ursula! . . . There is something the matter! . . .

QUEEN.

[*At the windows.*] Ursula! Ursula! . . . Pour some water on her! . . . —Yes, yes, do that, my child . . . It is perhaps not . . . ! Oh, oh, oh! . . . her little head! . . . [*Servitors, soldiers, peasants, women, run up on the terrace with torches and lanterns.*] Ursula! Ursula! . . . It is perhaps not that . . . It may be nothing at all! . . . Eh! eh! Claribel! Claribel! Take care! . . . She will fall! . . . Do not tread on her hair! . . . Open! open! — She will wake! she will wake! . . . water! water! water! — Open! open! the door! the door!

the door! . . . No one can get in! Everything is locked! everything is locked! . . . You are deaf as dead folk! . . . [*To those about her.*] Help me! — You are horrible people! My hands! . . . My hands! . . . You see my hands? . . . Help me! help me! Oh, oh! It is late! . . . It is too late? . . . It is too late! . . . closed! closed! closed! . . .

ALL.

[*Shaking the door and knocking at all the windows.*] Open! open! open! open! . . .
[A black curtain falls brusquely.]

The Death of Tintagiles.

To A. F. Lugné-Poe.

Persons.

TINTAGILES.
YGRAINE,
BELLANGÈRE, } *sisters of Tintagiles.*
AGLOVALE.
THREE SERVANTS OF THE QUEEN.

The Death of Tintagiles.

ACT FIRST.

At the top of a hill, overlooking the castle.

Enter YGRAINE, *holding* TINTAGILES *by the hand.*

YGRAINE.

Thy first night will be troubled, Tintagiles. Already the sea howls about us; and the trees are moaning. It is late. The moon is just setting behind the poplars that stifle the palace. . . . We are alone, perhaps, for all that here we have to live on guard. There seems to be a watch set for the approach of the slightest happiness. I said to myself one day, in the very depths of my soul, — and God himself could hardly hear it, — I said to myself one day I should be happy. . . . There needed nothing further; in a little while our old father died, and both our brothers vanished without a single human being able since to tell us where they are. Now I am all alone, with my poor sister and thee, my little Tintagiles; and I have no faith in the future. . . . Come here; sit on my knee. Kiss me first; and put thy little arms, there, all the way around my neck; . . . perhaps they will not be able to undo them. . . . Rememberest thou the time when it was I that carried thee at night when bedtime came; and when thou fearedst the shadows of my lamp in the long windowless corridors? — I felt my soul tremble upon my lips when I saw thee, suddenly, this morning. . . . I thought thee so far away, and so secure. . . . Who was it made thee come here?

TINTAGILES.

I do not know, little sister.

YGRAINE.

Thou dost not know any longer what was said?

TINTAGILES.

They said I had to leave.

YGRAINE.

But why hadst thou to leave?

TINTAGILES.

Because it was the Queen's will.

YGRAINE.

They did not say why it was her will? — I am sure they said many things. . . .

TINTAGILES.

I heard nothing, little sister.

YGRAINE.

When they spoke among themselves, what did they say?

TINTAGILES.

They spoke in a low voice, little sister.

YGRAINE.

All the time?

TINTAGILES.

All the time, sister Ygraine; except when they looked at me.

YGRAINE.

They did not speak of the Queen?

TINTAGILES.

They said she was never seen, sister Ygraine.

YGRAINE.

And those who were with thee, on the bridge of the ship, said nothing?

TINTAGILES.

They minded nothing but the wind and the sails, sister Ygraine.

YGRAINE.

Ah! . . . That does not astonish me, my child. . . .

TINTAGILES.

They left me all alone, little sister.

YGRAINE.

Listen, Tintagiles, I will tell thee what I know. . . .

TINTAGILES.

What dost thou know, sister Ygraine?

YGRAINE.

Not much, my child. . . . My sister and I have crept along here, since our birth, without daring to understand a whit of all that happens. . . . For a long while indeed, I lived like a blind woman on this island; and it all seemed natural to me. . . . I saw no other events than the flying of a bird, the trembling of a leaf, the opening of a rose. . . . There reigned such a silence that the falling of a ripe fruit in the park called faces to the windows. . . . And no one seemed to have the least suspicion; . . . but one night I learned there must be something else. . . . I would have fled, and could not. . . . Hast thou understood what I have said?

TINTAGILES.

Yes, yes, little sister; I understand whatever you will. . . .

YGRAINE.

Well, then, let us speak no more of things that are not known. . . . Thou seest yonder, behind the dead trees that poison the horizon, — thou seest the castle yonder, in the depth of the valley?

TINTAGILES.

That which is so black, sister Ygraine?

YGRAINE.

It is black indeed. . . . It is at the very depth of an amphitheatre of shadows. . . . We have to live there. . . . It might have been built on the summit of the great mountains that surround it. . . . The mountains are blue all day. . . . We should have breathed. We should have seen the sea and the meadows on the other side of the rocks. . . . But they preferred to put it in the depth of the valley; and the very air does not go down so low. . . . It is falling in ruins, and nobody bewares. . . . The walls are cracking; you would say it was dissolving in the shadows. . . . There is only one tower unassailed by the weather. . . . It is enormous; and the house never comes out of its shadow. . . .

TINTAGILES.

There is something shining, sister Ygraine. . . . See, see, the great red windows! . . .

YGRAINE.

They are those of the tower, Tintagiles: they are the only ones where you will see light; it is there the throne of the Queen is set.

TINTAGILES.

I shall not see the Queen?

YGRAINE.

No one can see her. . . .

TINTAGILES.

Why can't one see her?

YGRAINE.

Come nearer, Tintagiles. . . . Not a bird nor a blade of grass must hear us. . . .

TINTAGILES.

There is no grass, little sister. . . . [*A silence.*] — What does the Queen do?

YGRAINE.

No one knows, my child. She does not show herself. . . . She lives there, all alone in her tower; and they that serve her do not go out by day. . . . She is very old; she is the mother of our mother; and she would reign alone. . . . She is jealous and suspicious, and they say that she is mad. . . . She fears lest some one rise into her place; and it was doubtless because of that fear that she had thee brought hither. . . . Her orders are carried out no one knows how. . . . She never comes down; and all the doors of the tower are closed night and day. . . . I never caught a glimpse of her; but others have seen her, it seems, in the past, when she was young. . . .

TINTAGILES.

Is she very ugly, sister Ygraine?

YGRAINE.

They say she is not beautiful, and that she is growing huge. . . . But they that have seen her dare never speak of it. . . . Who knows, indeed, if they have seen her? . . . She has a power not to be understood; and we live here with a great unpitying weight upon our souls. . . . Thou must not be frightened beyond measure, nor have bad dreams; we shall watch over thee, my little Tintagiles, and no evil will be able to reach thee; but do not go far from me, your sister Bellangère, nor our old master Aglovale. . . .

TINTAGILES.

Not from Aglovale either, sister Ygraine?

YGRAINE.

Not from Aglovale either. . . . He loves us. . . .

TINTAGILES.

He is so old, little sister!

YGRAINE.

He is old, but very wise. . . . He is the only friend we have left; and he knows many things. . . . It is strange; she has made thee come hither without letting any one know. . . . I do not know what there is in my heart. . . . I was sorry and glad to know thou wert so far away, beyond the sea. . . . And now . . . I was astonished. . . . I went out this morning to see if the sun was rising over the mountains; and it is thou I see upon the threshold. . . . I knew thee at once. . . .

TINTAGILES.

No, no, little sister; it was I that laughed first. . . .

YGRAINE.

I could not laugh at once. . . . Thou wilt understand. . . . It is time, Tintagiles, and the wind is growing black upon the sea. . . . Kiss me harder, again, again, before thou stand'st upright. . . . Thou knowest not how we love. . . . Give me thy little hand. . . . I shall guard it well; and we will go back into the sickening castle.

[Exeunt.

ACT SECOND.

An apartment in the castle. AGLOVALE *and* YGRAINE *discovered.*

Enter BELLANGÈRE.

BELLANGÈRE.

Where is Tintagiles?

YGRAINE.

Here; do not speak too loud. He sleeps in the other room. He seems a little pale, a little ailing too. He was tired by the journey and the long sea-voyage. Or else the atmosphere of the castle has startled his little soul. He cried for no cause. I rocked him to sleep on my knees; come, see. . . . He sleeps in our bed. . . . He sleeps very gravely, with one hand on his forehead, like a little sad king. . . .

BELLANGÈRE (*bursting suddenly into tears*).

My sister! my sister! . . . my poor sister! . . .

YGRAINE.

What is the matter?

BELLANGÈRE.

I dare not say what I know, . . . and I am not sure that I know anything, . . . and yet I heard that which one could not hear. . . .

YGRAINE.

What didst thou hear?

BELLANGÈRE.

I was passing near the corridors of the tower. . . .

YGRAINE.

Ah! . . .

BELLANGÈRE.

A door there was ajar. I pushed it very softly. . . . I went in. . . .

YGRAINE.

In where?

BELLANGÈRE.

I had never seen the place. . . . There were other corridors lighted with lamps; then low galleries that had no outlet. . . . I knew it was forbidden to go on. . . . I was afraid, and I was going to return upon my steps, when I heard a sound of voices one could hardly hear. . . .

YGRAINE.

It must have been the handmaids of the Queen; they dwell at the foot of the tower. . . .

BELLANGÈRE.

I do not know just what it was. . . . There must have been more than one door between us; and the voices came to me like the voice of some one who was being smothered. . . . I drew as near as I could. . . . I am not sure of anything, but I think they spoke of a child that came to-day and of a crown of gold. . . . They seemed to be laughing. . . .

YGRAINE.

They laughed?

BELLANGÈRE.

Yes, I think they laughed . . . unless they were weeping, or unless it was something I did not understand; for it was hard to hear, and their voices were sweet. . . . They seemed to echo in a crowd under the arches. . . . They spoke of the child the Queen would see. . . . They will probably come up this evening. . . .

YGRAINE.

What? . . . This evening? . . .

BELLANGÈRE.

Yes. . . . Yes. . . . I think so. . . .

YGRAINE.

They spoke no one's name?

BELLANGÈRE.

They spoke of a child, of a very little child. . . .

YGRAINE.

There is no other child. . . .

BELLANGÈRE.

They raised their voices a little at that moment, because one of them had said the day seemed not yet come. . . .

YGRAINE.

I know what that means; it is not the first time they have issued from the tower. . . . I knew well why she made him come; . . . but I could not believe she would hasten so! . . . We shall see; . . . we are three, and we have time. . . .

BELLANGÈRE.

What wilt thou do?

YGRAINE.

I do not know yet what I shall do, but I will astonish her. . . . Do you know how you tremble? . . . I will tell you. . . .

BELLANGÈRE.

What?

YGRAINE.

She shall not take him without trouble. . . .

BELLANGÈRE.

We are alone, sister Ygraine. . . .

YGRAINE.

Ah! it is true, we are alone! . . . There is but one remedy, the one with which we have always succeeded! . . . Let us wait upon our knees as the other times. . . . Perhaps she will have pity! . . . She allows herself to be disarmed by tears. . . . We must grant her all she asks us; haply she will smile; and she is wont to spare all those who kneel. . . . She has been there for years in her huge tower, devouring our beloved, and none, not one, has dared to strike her in the face. . . . She is there, upon our souls, like the stone of a tomb, and no one dare put forth his arm. . . . In the time when there were men here, they feared too, and fell upon their faces. . . . To-day it is the woman's turn; . . . we shall see. . . . It is time to rise at last. . . . We know not upon what her power rests, and I will live no longer in the shadow of her tower. . . . Go, — go, both of you, and leave me more alone still, if you tremble too. . . . I shall await her. . . .

BELLANGÈRE.

Sister, I do not know what must be done, but I stay with thee. . . .

AGLOVALE.

I too stay, my daughter. For a long time my soul has been restless. . . . You are going to try. . . . We have tried more than once. . . .

The Death of Tintagiles.

YGRAINE.

You have tried . . . you too?

AGLOVALE.

They have all tried. . . . But at the last moment they have lost their strength. . . . You will see, you too. . , . Should she order me to come up to her this very night, I should clasp both my hands without a word; and my tired feet would climb the stair, without delay and without haste, well as I know no one comes down again with open eyes. . . . I have no more courage against her. . . . Our hands are of no use and reach no one. . . . They are not the hands we need, and all is useless. . . . But I would help you, because you hope. . . . Shut the doors, my child. Wake Tintagiles; encircle him with your little naked arms and take him on your knees. . . . We have no other defence. . . .

ACT THIRD.

The same. YGRAINE *and* AGLOVALE *discovered.*

YGRAINE.

I have been to all the doors. There are three. We will guard the largest. . . . The other two are thick and low. They never open. Their keys were lost long ago, and the iron bars are bedded fast in the walls. Help me shut this; it is heavier than the gate of a city. . . . It is strong, too, and the thunder itself could not enter. . . Are you ready for everything?

AGLOVALE (*seating himself on the threshold*).

I shall sit on the steps of the threshold, with the sword on my knees. . . . Methinks it is not the first time I have watched and waited here, my child; and there are moments when we do not understand all we remember. . . . I have done these things, I know not when; . . . but I never dared draw my sword. . . . To-day it is there, before me, although my arms have no more strength; but I will try. . . . Perhaps it is time to defend ourselves, although we do not understand. . . .

BELLANGÈRE, *carrying* TINTAGILES, *enters from the adjoining room.*

BELLANGÈRE.

He was awake. . . .

YGRAINE.

He is pale. . . . Why, what is the matter?

BELLANGÈRE.

I do not know. . . . He was crying silently. . . .

YGRAINE.

Tintagiles. . . .

BELLANGÈRE.

He looks the other way. . . .

YGRAINE.

He does not recognize me. . . . Tintagiles, where art thou? — It is thy sister speaking to thee. . . . What lookest thou at there? — Turn back this way. . . . Come, we will play. . . .

TINTAGILES.

No. . . . No. . . .

YGRAINE.

Thou wouldst not play?

TINTAGILES.

I can no longer walk, sister Ygraine. . . .

YGRAINE.

Thou canst no longer walk? . . . Come, come, what ails thee? — Art thou in pain a little? . . .

TINTAGILES.

Yes. . . .

YGRAINE.

Where is the pain, then? — Tell me, Tintagiles, and I will cure thee. . . .

TINTAGILES.

I can't tell, sister Ygraine, it is everywhere. . . .

YGRAINE.

Come here, Tintagiles. . . . Thou knowest my arms are gentler, and one is cured quickly there. . . . Give him to me, Bellangère. . . . He shall sit on my knees, and it will go away. . . . There, thou seest how it is! . . . Thy great sisters are here. . . . They are about thee; . . . we will defend thee, and no harm can come. . . .

TINTAGILES.

It is there, sister Ygraine. . . . Why is there no light, sister Ygraine?

YGRAINE.

There is, my child. . . . Thou dost not see the lamp that hangs down from the vault?

TINTAGILES.

Yes, yes. . . . It is not big. . . . There are no others?

YGRAINE.

Why should there be others? We can see all we need see. . . .

TINTAGILES.

Ah ! . . .

YGRAINE.

Oh, thine eyes are deep ! . . .

TINTAGILES.

Thine too, sister Ygraine. . . .

YGRAINE.

I had not noticed it this morning. . . . I saw arise . . . one never knows just what the soul believes it sees. . . .

TINTAGILES.

I have not seen the soul, sister Ygraine. . . . Why is Aglovale there on the threshold?

YGRAINE.

He is resting a little. . . . He wanted to kiss thee before he went to bed. . . . He was waiting for thee to wake. . . .

TINTAGILES.

What is that on his knees?

YGRAINE.

On his knees? I see nothing on his knees. . . .

The Death of Tintagiles.

TINTAGILES.

Yes, yes, there is something. . . .

AGLOVALE.

Nothing much, my child. . . . I was looking at my old sword; and I hardly recognized it. . . . It has served me many years; but for some time I have lost all faith in it, and I think it will soon break. . . . There, by the hilt, there is a little spot. . . . I have observed the steel was growing paler, and I asked myself . . . I know not any longer what I asked. . . . My soul is very heavy to-day. . . . How can it be helped? . . . We have to live in expectation of the unexpected. . . . And then we have to act as if we hoped. . . . There are those heavy evenings when the uselessness of life rises in the throat; and you would like to close your eyes. . . . It is late, and I am tired. . . .

TINTAGILES.

He is wounded, sister Ygraine. . . .

YGRAINE.

Where?

TINTAGILES.

On the forehead and the hands. . . .

AGLOVALE.

Those are very old wounds that do not hurt me any more, my child. . . . It must be the light falling on them to-night. . . . Thou hast never noticed them till now?

TINTAGILES.

He looks sad, sister Ygraine. . . .

YGRAINE.

No, no; he is not sad, but very weary. . . .

TINTAGILES.

Thou art sad too, sister Ygraine. . . .

YGRAINE.

Why, no; why, no; you see, I am smiling. . . .

TINTAGILES.

And my other sister, too. . . .

YGRAINE.

Why, no; she is smiling, too. . . .

TINTAGILES.

That is not smiling. . . . I know. . . .

YGRAINE.

Come; kiss me and think of something else. . . . [*She kisses him.*]

TINTAGILES.

What else, sister Ygraine? — Why dost thou hurt me when thou dost kiss me so?

YGRAINE.

I hurt thee?

The Death of Tintagiles.

TINTAGILES.

Yes. . . . I don't know why I hear thy heart beat, sister Ygraine. . . .

YGRAINE.

Thou hearest it beat?

TINTAGILES.

Oh! oh! it beats, it beats, as if it would . . .

YGRAINE.

What?

TINTAGILES.

I don't know, sister Ygraine. . . .

YGRAINE.

Thou must not be alarmed without reason, nor speak in riddles. . . . Stop! thine eyes are wet. . . . Why art thou troubled? I hear thy heart beat, too. . . . You always hear it when you kiss so. . . . It is then it speaks and says things the tongue knows not of. . . .

TINTAGILES.

I did not hear it just now. . . .

YGRAINE.

Because then . . . Oh! but thine! . . . Why, what ails it? . . . It is bursting! . . .

TINTAGILES (*crying*).

Sister Ygraine! sister Ygraine!

YGRAINE.

What?

TINTAGILES.

I heard! . . . They . . . they are coming!

YGRAINE.

They, who? . . . Why, what's the matter? . . .

TINTAGILES.

The door! the door! They were there! . . .
[*He falls backward on* YGRAINE'S *knees.*

YGRAINE.

Why, what's the matter? . . . He has . . . he has fainted. . . .

BELLANGÈRE.

Take care; . . . take care! . . . He will fall. . . .

AGLOVALE.

[*Rising abruptly, sword in hand.*] I hear too; . . . some one is walking in the corridor.

YGRAINE.

Oh! . . .

[*A silence — they listen.*

AGLOVALE.

I hear. . . . There is a crowd of them. . . .

YGRAINE.

A crowd! . . . What crowd?

AGLOVALE.

I do not know; . . . you hear and you do not hear. . . . They do not walk like other beings, but they come. . . . They are touching the door. . . .

YGRAINE.

[*Clasping* TINTAGILES *convulsively in her arms.*] Tintagiles! . . . Tintagiles! . . .

BELLANGÈRE.

[*Kissing him at the same time.*] I too! . . . I too! . . . Tintagiles! . . .

AGLOVALE.

They are shaking the door . . . listen . . . soft! . . . They are whispering. . . .
[*A key is heard grating in the lock.*

YGRAINE.

They have the key! . . .

AGLOVALE.

Yes; . . . yes. . . . I was sure of it. . . . Wait. . . .
[*He posts himself, with raised sword, on the last step. — To the two sisters :*]
Come! . . . come, too! . . .
[A silence. The door opens a little. Trembling like the needle of a compass, Aglovale puts his sword across the opening, sticking the point of it between the beams of the door-case. The sword breaks with a crash under the ominous pressure of the folding-

door, and its fragments roll echoing down the steps. Ygraine leaps up with Tintagiles, still in a faint, in her arms; and she, Bellangère and Aglovale, with vain and mighty efforts, try to push back the door, which continues to open slowly, although no one is heard or seen. Only a brightness, cold and calm, pierces into the room. At this moment, Tintagiles, suddenly straightening up, comes to himself, utters a long cry of deliverance and kisses his sister, while at the very moment of this cry, the door, resisting no longer, shuts abruptly under their pressure, which they have not had time to interrupt.]

YGRAINE.

Tintagiles! . . .

[*They look at each other in amazement.*

AGLOVALE (*listening at the door*).

I no longer hear a sound. . . .

YGRAINE (*wild with joy*).

Tintagiles! Tintagiles! . . . See! See! . . . He is saved! . . . See his eyes! . . . you can see the blue. . . . He is going to speak. . . . They saw we were watching. . . . They did not dare! . . . Kiss us! . . . Kiss us, I tell thee! . . . Kiss us! . . . All! all! . . . To the very depths of our souls! . . .

[*All four, with eyes filled with tears, remain closely embraced.*]

ACT FOURTH.

[A corridor before the apartment of the preceding act. Enter, veiled, three handmaids of the Queen.]

FIRST HANDMAID (*listening at the door*).

They watch no longer. . . .

SECOND HANDMAID.

It was useless to wait. . . .

THIRD HANDMAID.

She preferred that it should be done in silence. . . .

FIRST HANDMAID.

I knew that they must sleep. . . .

SECOND HANDMAID.

Open quickly. . . .

THIRD HANDMAID.

It is time. . . .

FIRST HANDMAID.

Wait at the door. I will go in alone. It is needless to be three. . . .

SECOND HANDMAID.

It is true, he is very little. . . .

THIRD HANDMAID.

You must be on your guard for the elder sister. . . .

SECOND HANDMAID.

You know the Queen would not that they should know. . . .

FIRST HANDMAID.

Fear nothing; I am never easily heard. . . .

SECOND HANDMAID.

Go in, then; it is time.
  [*The first handmaid opens the door prudently and enters the room.*]

It is nearly midnight. . . .

THIRD HANDMAID.

Ah! . . .
  [*A silence. The first handmaid comes back from the apartment.*]

SECOND HANDMAID.

Where is he?

FIRST HANDMAID.

He is asleep between his sisters. His arms are about their necks; and their arms are about him, too. . . . I could not do it alone. . . .

SECOND HANDMAID.

I will go help you. . . .

THIRD HANDMAID.

Yes; go in together. . . . I will watch here. . . .

FIRST HANDMAID.

Take care; they are aware of something. . . . They are all three struggling with a bad dream. . . .

[*The two handmaids enter the room.*

THIRD HANDMAID.

They are always aware; but they do not understand. . . .

[*A silence. The first two handmaids come back again from the apartment.*]

Well?

SECOND HANDMAID.

You must come too; . . . we cannot detach them. . . .

FIRST HANDMAID.

As fast as we undo their arms, they close them on the child again. . . .

SECOND HANDMAID.

And the child clings to them harder and harder. . . .

FIRST HANDMAID.

He is resting with his forehead on the elder sister's heart. . . .

SECOND HANDMAID.

And his head rises and falls on her breasts. . . .

FIRST HANDMAID.

We shall not succeed in opening his hands the least. . . .

SECOND HANDMAID.

They plunge to the very depths of his sisters' hair. . . .

FIRST HANDMAID.

He clenches a golden curl between his little teeth. . . .

SECOND HANDMAID.

The hair of the elder will have to be cut off. . . .

FIRST HANDMAID.

The other sister's as well, you will see. . . .

SECOND HANDMAID.

Have you your shears?

THIRD HANDMAID.

Yes. . . .

FIRST HANDMAID.

Come quick; they stir already.

SECOND HANDMAID.

Their hearts and eyelids beat in the same time. . . .

FIRST HANDMAID.

It is true; I caught a glimpse of the blue eyes of the elder. . . .

SECOND HANDMAID.

She looked at us, but saw us not. . . .

FIRST HANDMAID.

When one of them is touched, the other two start. . . .

SECOND HANDMAID.

They struggle without being able to move. . . .

FIRST HANDMAID.

The elder would have cried out, but she could not. . . .

SECOND HANDMAID.

Come quickly; they look warned. . . .

THIRD HANDMAID.

The old man is not there?

FIRST HANDMAID.

Yes; but he sleeps in a corner. . . .

SECOND HANDMAID.

He sleeps with his forehead on the pommel of his sword.

FIRST HANDMAID.

He is aware of nothing; and he does not dream. . . .

THIRD HANDMAID.

Come, come; we must have done with it. . . .

FIRST HANDMAID.

You will have trouble untangling their limbs. . . .

SECOND HANDMAID.

True; they are intertwined like those of the drowned. . . .

THIRD HANDMAID.

Come, come. . . .

[They enter the room. A great silence, broken by sighs and dull murmurs of an anguish smothered by sleep. Afterwards, the three handmaids come out in all haste from the sombre apartment. One of them carries Tintagiles asleep in her arms, his little hands and mouth shrivelled with sleep and agony, and flooding him all over with the flowing of long golden locks ravished from the two sisters' hair. They flee in silence until, when they come to the end of the corridor, Tintagiles, suddenly waking, utters a great cry of supreme distress.]

TINTAGILES (*from the depths of the corridor*).

A-ah ! . . .

[New silence. Then the two sisters are heard, in the next room, waking and rising uneasily.]

YGRAINE (*in the room*).

Tintagiles! . . . Where is he? . . .

BELLANGÈRE.

He is no longer here. . . .

YGRAINE (*with increasing anguish*).

Tintagiles ! . . . A lamp ! a lamp ! . . . Light it ! . . .

BELLANGÈRE.

Yes . . . yes ! . . .

YGRAINE.

[She is seen, through the open door, coming forward within the room, with a lamp in her hand.]

The door is wide open !

THE VOICE OF TINTAGILES (*almost inaudible in the distance*).

Sister Ygraine ! . . .

YGRAINE.

He cries ! . . . he cries ! . . . Tintagiles ! Tintagiles ! . . .

[She rushes headlong into the corridor. Bellangère tries to follow her, but faints on the steps of the threshold.]

ACT FIFTH.

A great iron door beneath gloomy arches. Enter YGRAINE, *haggard, dishevelled, with a lamp in her hand.*

YGRAINE.

[*Turning back wildly.*] They have not followed me. . . . Bellangère ! . . . Bellangère ! . . . Aglovale ! . . . Where are they? — They said they loved him, and they have left me all alone ! . . . Tintagiles ! . . . Tintagiles ! . . . Oh ! it is true. . . . I have climbed up, I have climbed up innumerable steps between great pitiless walls, and my heart can no longer sustain me. . . . The arches seem to stir. . . . [*She leans against the pillars of an arch.*] I shall fall. . . . Oh ! oh ! my poor life ! I feel it. . . . It is at the very edge of my lips, trying to get away. . . . I do not know what I have done. . . . I have seen nothing ; I have heard nothing. . . . Oh, the silence ! . . . I found all these golden curls along the steps and along the walls ; and I followed them. I picked them up. . . . Oh ! oh ! they are very beautiful ! Little thumbkin ! . . . little thumbkin ! . . . What did I say? I remember. . . . I do not believe in it, either ; . . . one can sleep. . . . All that is of no consequence, and it is not possible. . . . I do not know what I think any longer. . . . One is waked up, and then . . . At bottom, come, at bottom, one must reflect. . . . They say this, they say that; but the soul — that follows another road altogether. You do not know all you unloose. I came here with my little lamp. . . . It was not blown out in spite of the wind in the stairway. . . . At bottom, what must be thought of it? There are too many things unsettled. . . . And yet there are some who should know them; but why do they not speak? [*Looking about her.*] I have never seen all this. . . . One may not climb so high; everything is forbidden. . . . It is cold. . . . It is so dark, too, one might fear to breathe. . . . They say the shadows poison. . . . Yonder door is fearful. . . . [*She approaches the door and gropes over it.*] Oh! it is cold! . . . It is of smooth iron; all smooth, and has no lock. . . . Where does it open, then? I see no hinges. . . . I believe it is embedded in the wall. . . . One can go no higher; . . . there are no more steps. . . . [*Uttering a terrible cry.*] Ah! . . . still more golden curls, shut in the door! . . . Tintagiles! Tintagiles! . . . I heard the door fall to just now! . . . I remember! I remember! . . . It must! . . . [*She beats frantically with fist and feet on the door.*] Oh! the monster! the monster! . . . You are here! . . . Listen! I blaspheme! I blaspheme and spit at you! . . .

    [Knocking, in tiny strokes, heard on the other side of the door; then the voice of Tintagiles pierces, very feebly, through the iron barriers.]

TINTAGILES.

Sister Ygraine, sister Ygraine!

YGRAINE.

Tintagiles! . . . What? . . . What? . . . Tintagiles, is it thou? . . .

TINTAGILES.

Open quickly, open quickly! . . . She is there! . . .

YGRAINE.

Oh! oh! . . . Who? . . . Tintagiles, my little Tintagiles! . . . dost thou hear me? . . . What is it! . . . What has happened? . . . Tintagiles! . . . Thou hast not been hurt? . . . Where art thou? . . . Art thou there? . . .

TINTAGILES.

Sister Ygraine, sister Ygraine! . . . I shall die if thou dost not open me the door. . . .

YGRAINE.

Wait; I am trying; wait. . . . I am opening it, I am opening it. . . .

TINTAGILES.

But thou dost not understand me! . . . Sister Ygraine! . . . There is no time! . . . She could not hold me. . . . I struck her, struck her. . . . I ran. . . . Quick, quick, she is here! . . .

YGRAINE.

I am coming, I am coming. . . . Where is she?

TINTAGILES.

I see nothing, . . . but I hear . . . oh ! I am afraid, sister Ygraine, I am afraid ! . . . Quick, quick ! . . . Open quickly ! . . . for the love of the dear God, sister Ygraine ! . . .

YGRAINE (*groping over the door anxiously*).

I am sure to find . . . wait a little . . . a minute . . . a moment . . .

TINTAGILES.

I cannot wait any longer, sister Ygraine. . . . She is breathing behind me. . . .

YGRAINE.

It is nothing, Tintagiles; my little Tintagiles, don't be afraid. . . . It is because I cannot see. . . .

TINTAGILES.

Yes, thou canst; I see thy light plainly. . . . It is light by thee, sister Ygraine. . . . Here I can see no longer. . . .

YGRAINE.

Thou seest me, Tintagiles? Where can one see? There is no chink. . . .

TINTAGILES.

Yes, yes, there is one, but it is so little ! . . .

YGRAINE

Which side? Here? . . . Tell me, tell me ! . . . There, perhaps ?

TINTAGILES.

Here, here. . . . Dost thou not hear? I am knocking. . . .

YGRAINE.

Here?

TINTAGILES.

Higher. . . . But it is so little! . . . One could not pass a needle through it! . . .

YGRAINE.

Don't be afraid; I shall be there. . . .

TINTAGILES.

Oh, I hear, sister Ygraine! . . . Pull! Pull! Thou must pull! She is here! . . . if thou couldst open it a little . . . just a little. . . . I am so tiny! . . .

YGRAINE.

I have no nails left, Tintagiles. . . . I have pulled, I have pushed, I have pounded! . . . I have pounded! . . . [*She pounds again and tries to shake the immovable door.*] Two of my fingers are numb. . . . Do not weep; . . . it is iron. . . .

TINTAGILES (*sobbing desperately*).

Thou hast nothing to open it with, sister Ygraine? . . . Nothing at all, nothing at all; . . . and I could go through; . . . for I am so little, so little. . . . Thou knowest well. . . .

YGRAINE.

I have nothing but my lamp, Tintagiles. . . . There! There! . . . [*She beats hard on the door, with the help of her lamp of clay, which goes out and is broken.*] Oh ! . . . Everything is dark all at once ! . . . Tintagiles, where art thou ? . . . Oh, listen, listen ! . . . Thou canst not open it from within ? . . .

TINTAGILES.

No, no ; there is n't anything. . . . I can't feel anything at all. . . . I can't see the little bright chink any longer. . . .

YGRAINE.

What ails thee, Tintagiles ? . . . I hardly hear any longer. . . .

TINTAGILES.

Little sister, sister Ygraine. . . . It is no longer possible. . . .

YGRAINE.

What is it, Tintagiles ? . . . Where goest thou ? . . .

TINTAGILES.

She is there ! . . . I have no more courage. — Sister Ygraine, sister Ygraine ! . . . I feel her ! . . .

YGRAINE.

Who ? . . . Who ? . . .

TINTAGILES.

I do not know. . . . I do not see. . . . But it is no longer possible ! . . . She . . . she is taking me by the throat. . . . She has put her hand on my throat. . . . Oh ! oh ! sister Ygraine, come here. . . .

YGRAINE.

Yes, yes. . . .

TINTAGILES.

It is so dark ! . . .

YGRAINE.

Struggle, defend thyself, tear her ! . . . Don't be afraid. . . . One moment ! . . . I shall be there. . . . Tintagiles ! . . . Tintagiles ! answer me ! . . . Help ! . . . Where art thou ? . . . I am going to help thee. . . . Kiss me . . . through the door . . . here . . . here. . . .

TINTAGILES (*very feebly*).

Here . . . here . . . sister Ygraine. . . .

YGRAINE.

It is here, it is here I am giving kisses, hearest thou ? Again ! again ! . . .

TINTAGILES (*more and more feebly*).

I am giving them, too . . . here . . . sister Ygraine ! . . . sister Ygraine ! . . . Oh ! . . .
[*The fall of a little body is heard behind the iron door.*]

YGRAINE.

Tintagiles ! . . . Tintagiles ! . . . What hast thou done ? . . . Give him up ! give him up ! . . . for the love of God, give him up ! . . . I no longer hear. . . . — What have you done with him ? . . . Do him no harm, will you ? . . . It is only a poor child ! . . . He does not resist. . . . See, see. . . . I am not wicked. . . . I have gone down on both knees. . . . Give him up, I pray thee. . . . It is not for myself alone, thou knowest. . . . I will do all one could wish. . . . I am not bad, you see. . . . I beseech you with clasped hands. . . . I was wrong. . . . I submit utterly, thou seest well. . . . I have lost all I had. . . . Let me be punished some other way. . . . There are so many things that could give me more pain . . . if thou lovest to give pain . . . . Thou wilt see. . . . But this poor child has done nothing. . . . What I said was not true . . . but I did not know. . . . I know well you are very good. . . . One must forgive in the end ! . . . He is so young, he is so beautiful, and he is so little ! . . . You see, it is not possible ! . . . He puts his little arms about your neck, his little mouth on your mouth ; and God himself could not resist any longer. . . . You will open, will you not ? . . . I ask almost nothing. . . . I should only have him a moment, one little moment. . . . I do not remember . . . thou understandest. . . . I did not have time. . . . There needs hardly anything to let him pass. . . . It is not hard. . . . [*A long inexorable silence.*] — Monster ! . . . Monster ! . . . I spit —. . . !

    [*She sinks down and continues to sob softly, with her arms stretched up on the door, in the darkness.*]

[CURTAIN.]

University of California
SOUTHERN REGIONAL LIBRARY FACILITY
305 De Neve Drive - Parking Lot 17 • Box 951388
LOS ANGELES, CALIFORNIA 90095-1388
Return this material to the library from which it was borrowed.

NOV 07

Book

UCLA-College Library
PQ 2624 A5I6E

ImTheStory.com

Personalized Classic Books in many genre's

Unique gift for kids, partners, friends, colleagues

Customize:
- Character Names
- Upload your own front/back cover images (optional)
- Inscribe a personal message/dedication on the inside page (optional)

Customize many titles Including
- Alice in Wonderland
- Romeo and Juliet
- The Wizard of Oz
- A Christmas Carol
- Dracula
- Dr. Jekyll & Mr. Hyde
- And more...